Political Innovation
in America

Political Innovation in America

THE POLITICS OF POLICY INITIATION

Nelson W. Polsby

Yale University Press
New Haven and London

Published with assistance from the Stern Memorial Fund.

Designed by Nancy Ovedovitz and set in Caledonia type. Printed in the United States of America by Halliday Lithograph, West Hanover, Massachusetts.

Library of Congress Cataloging in Publication Data

Polsby, Nelson W.
Political innovation in America.
Includes index.
1. United States—Politics and government—1945–
2. Diffusion of innovations—United States.   3. Policy sciences.   I. Title.
JK271.P567   1984   320.973   83–14749
ISBN 0–300–03089–4

10   9   8   7   6   5   4   3   2   1

For Linda,
Lisa, Emily, and Dan

My part was to bring in Bills already prepared, and to sustain the discussion of them during the short time they were allowed to remain before the House; after having taken an active part in the work of a Committee . . . which sat through the greater part of the Session . . . to take evidence on the subject. The very different position in which the question now stands . . . may justly be attributed to the preparation which went on during those years, and which produced but little visible effect at the time; . . . all questions on which there are strong private interests on one side, and only the public good on the other, have a similar period of incubation to go through.

—John Stuart Mill, *Autobiography*

Many who before regarded legislation on the subject as chimerical, will now fancy that it is only dangerous, or perhaps not more than difficult. And so in time it will come to be looked on as among the things possible, then among the things probable;—and so at last it will be ranged in the list of those few measures which the country requires as being absolutely needed. That is the way public opinion is made.

—Anthony Trollope, *Phineas Finn*

As for policy . . . it must be said, as it has been said of sovereignty, that its real sources are undiscoverable.

—Dean Acheson, *Grapes from Thorns*

[T]he ideas of economists and political philosophers, both when they are right and when they are wrong, are more powerful than is commonly understood. Indeed the world is ruled by little else. Practical men, who believe themselves to be quite exempt from any intellectual influences, are usually the slaves of some defunct economist. Madmen in authority, who hear voices in the air, are distilling their frenzy from some academic scribbler of a few years back.

—John Maynard Keynes, *The General Theory of Employment, Interest, and Money*

Contents

Preface

Optimists, it is commonly reported, contemplate the doughnut; pessimists, the hole. Attractive and plausible as this formula seems at first blush, it does not entirely accord with experience. Persons who are to any degree reflective about the buzzing, blooming confusion of life around them develop expectations; it is the violation of these expectations, and the consequent creation of anomalies, that quite properly draws and holds their attention.[1] Thus, for an inquiring optimist, whose world is full of doughnuts, it is holes that need explaining; a thoughtful pessimist, contrariwise, grapples to understand the appearance of life's occasional doughnut.

A study of policies that are in one way or another eventually enacted is about doughnuts and thus will probably appeal more to pessimistic than optimistic readers. Optimists who study American government have readily available more than enough material with which to gratify their taste for anomaly. The daily disasters of the morning newspaper aside, the literature describing obdurate congressional committees, venal or helpless regulatory agencies, slack or officious bureaucrats, autocratic or interfering judges, selfish politicians, and so forth is easily to hand for the benefit of those who wish to gorge themselves on reasons why good things are done so seldom and bad things are done so often. My own ever-subtler contributions to this burgeoning art form I leave to other occasions. In these pages I hope to pursue a different tack, asking how it happens that new

---

1. Some support for this notion may be found in accounts of scientific activity such as Thomas Kuhn's otherwise controversial *The Structure of Scientific Revolutions* (Chicago: University of Chicago Press, 1962). Even if this were not the case, I would not think of violating an important norm of contemporary political science by neglecting to cite this book at the earliest opportunity.

policies— political innovations—are initiated in the American political system.

I have in the course of this research incurred unusual debts. For reasons outlined a little farther on, I believe it is necessary to adopt the strategy of assembling a number of case studies and inspecting them synoptically for clues about the sources of policy innovation. This has entailed entering a large and disparate number of empirical domains, cutting through irrelevancies copiously strewn in the way, seizing hold of the main facts about policy initiation, and reporting them as succinctly as justice to the subject matter will permit. I doubt that I could have accomplished this single-handedly in the eight cases to be presented here—or in any sizable number of instances—within a reasonable time or without losing entirely the thread of my more general inquiry. Thus it gives me particular pleasure to acknowledge my good fortune in having had as collaborators in the original assembly of the case materials three graduate students who worked with great sensitivity and dispatch.

The earliest drafts of each of the case studies were written from published sources at my request in 1969 by Samuel H. Kernell. These I edited, sometimes heavily, sometimes lightly, and rewrote. They were then more comprehensively studied and once again recast by William Cavala or Byron Shafer before I gave them another going-over. To each of these colleagues I owe a great deal, as I do to the Center for the Study of Law and Society and the Institute of International Studies at Berkeley, whose support made it possible for me to employ them. The Ford Foundation, through a faculty research fellowship in 1970—71, gave me the time I needed to work on these materials myself, and a grant from the University of California Committee on Research helped me put further work into this manuscript.

I would also like to give public thanks to the now defunct Committee on Governmental and Legal Processes of the Social Science Research Council and to the moving spirit of the Council for many years, Pendleton Herring. This immensely useful committee grubstaked my early scholarly explorations into American national politics and kept the study of American government alive for many of us at a time when it was much out of fashion. Now, when the problems and promises of politics in America are on everybody's mind, one hopes that the intellectual standards that the Committee promoted are not forgotten.

Kathleen Peters with unflagging good humor typed the early drafts of the manuscript and kept at bay the mail and all the other odds and ends that drifted into my office. At a time when these became truly formidable, I was fortunate to have the secretarial help of Barbara Hight (now Barbara Kelly) and the research assistance of Steven Van Evera, which enabled me to complete a draft of this essay.

All this work was done between 1969 and 1972. I then set the manuscript aside and became engaged in other things, hoping to work on shortcomings in the presentation in due course. Due course finally arrived ten years later, owing to my good fortune in having the stimulating company of two skilled research assistants, Michael Goldstein and Peverill Squire, and the encouragement of colleagues who for one reason or another had heard of the existence of a manuscript on policy initiation. Former students who had once read it or, in Byron Shafer's case, worked on it also urged me to pull the manuscript off the shelf and see how well it had aged.

I was surprised to see that it had not aged badly and that I could even make use of the good suggestions, still preserved in a box in my study, that friends had made about earlier versions. For their thoughtfulness, time, and trouble over ten years ago, it gives me great pleasure to thank in particular Robert Axelrod, Aaron Wildavsky, Eugene Bardach, Serge Taylor, Arthur Stinchcombe, Charles O. Jones, Richard F. Fenno, and John Manley, who were one and all constructive and helpful. I also appreciate the work of members of the *American Political Science Review* editorial interns' seminar, who gave a partial draft a thorough going-over, and that of Mark Westlye and Steven Rosenstone, who called relevant materials to my attention.

More recently I have had the help of knowledgeable colleagues in forestalling some errors in the presentation of the case material. Edwin Bayley read the Peace Corps section, Richard Abrams the sections on the Truman Doctrine and the Council of Economic Advisers, John Heilbron the science cases, Russell D. Murphy the account of the origins of the Community Action Program, and Theodore R. Marmor the discussion of Medicare. Readers of the new version of the manuscript to whom I am particularly grateful include

John Hart, Michael Kraft, Robert K. Merton, and Aaron Wildavsky. Of course I am responsible for the mistakes they have been unsuccessful in persuading me to remove. I have also, as is my incorrigible custom, tried out some of the ideas contained here in occasional papers.[2]

Because Linda, Lisa, Emily, and Daniel Polsby are my favorite people in all the world, I like to put their names into my prefaces. I have no idea what they contributed to the writing of this book, unless it was me.

                                                             N. W. P.

Berkeley, California
August 8, 1983

---

2. One was originally delivered as a talk at the conference marking the founding of the Graduate School of Public Policy at the University of California, Berkeley, in November 1969 and subsequently published as "Policy Initiation in the American Political System," in Irving Louis Horowitz, ed., *The Use and Abuse of Social Science* (New Brunswick, N.J.: Transaction Books, 1971), pp. 296–308. Others were "Strengthening Congress in National Policy-Making," *Yale Review* 59 (June 1970): 481–497, and "Policy Analysis and Congress," *Public Policy* 18 (Fall 1969): 61–74.

I
Introduction

1. THE QUESTION POSED: THE POLITICS OF ENACTMENT, ADMINISTRATION, AND INITIATION

This essay attempts a brief overview of American national politics from a single, narrow perspective, that of policy initiation. It asks a purposely naive question: Where do new public policies come from?

We hear a great deal these days about the need for "new" policy—new priorities, new ideas, new departures. We hear practically nothing at all, however, about how new policies are to be brought into being. If we assume, as I think prudent, that today's new policies, when and if they emerge, are likely to come about in ways not unlike the ways in which new policies were born in the past, the study of past policy initiation can serve in a small way as a road map to the future. Conceivably, it can also assist those who want to initiate new policies by forestalling the misdirection of their resources and pointing them toward paths that have led others to success.

For years students of American politics have been acutely aware of institutions and processes in their national life that periodically enacted, and failed to enact, policies into law. As legalistic views of the world have given way in political science to views that have comprehended practice as well as prescription, a progressive enrichment has taken place in our common understanding of legislative enactment— from the study of Congress alone to the interaction of Congress with the President, from solitary actors to busy interactors, from faceless occupants of legally defined positions to stars and second bananas, character actors and retinues of bit players: congressmen from right and left, interest groups and lobbyists, executive agencies and their lawyers, committee staffs, and so on.

Indeed, the process by which legislation is enacted has more than a

1

little of the theater about it: a very imposing setting, which facilitates entrances and exits, a linear structure, easily divisible into acts and scenes, and most helpful of all, a climax—the passage of a bill, followed by a ceremonial termination at which fountain pens are passed around among important people while flashbulbs pop.

It is understandable in the light of the dramatic possibilities that so many good studies of enactment politics have been done.[1] But, as we all know, in real life, unlike in the theater, after the limelight is turned off dramatis personae must continue to struggle on about their business. After a bill is enacted it must be appropriated for and administered, and these two processes may have fateful consequences in shaping and reshaping the policies originally passed into law. Students of policymaking have consequently not stopped at the study of enactment. They have inquired about the administration of public policy, the discretion of administrators, and other determinants of variations in the enforcement, application, and implementation of general laws.[2]

Studying the administration of law is no simple matter. The pro-

---

1. See, for example, Stephen K. Bailey, *Congress Makes a Law* (New York: Columbia University Press, 1950); Daniel M. Berman, *A Bill Becomes a Law* (New York: Macmillan, 1962); H. Douglas Price, "Race, Religion, and the Rules Committee," in Alan F. Westin, ed., *The Uses of Power* (New York: Harcourt, Brace, and World, 1962), pp. 1–71; Robert Bendiner, *Obstacle Course on Capitol Hill* (New York: McGraw-Hill, 1964); Eugene Eidenberg and Roy D. Morey, *An Act of Congress: The Legislative Process and the Making of Education Policy* (New York: Norton, 1969); Robert L. Peabody, Jeffrey M. Berry, William G. Frasure, and Jerry Goldman, *To Enact a Law: Congress and Campaign Financing* (New York: Praeger, 1972); Eric Redman, *The Dance of Legislation* (New York: Simon and Schuster, 1973); Gary Orfield, *Congressional Power: Congress and Social Change* (New York: Harcourt Brace Jovanovich, 1974), pp. 61–250; and T. R. Reid, *Congressional Odyssey: The Saga of a Senate Bill* (San Francisco: W. H. Freeman, 1980).

2. See Harold C. Stein, *Public Administration and Policy Development* (New York: Harcourt, Brace and Co., 1952); Stephen K. Bailey and Edith K. Mosher, *ESEA: The Office of Education Administers a Law* (Syracuse: Syracuse University Press, 1968); Jeffrey L. Pressman and Aaron B. Wildavsky, *Implementation* (Berkeley and Los Angeles: University of California Press, 1973); Eugene Bardach, *The Implementation Game* (Cambridge: MIT Press, 1977); Robert A. Kagan, *Regulatory Justice* (New York: Russell Sage Foundation, 1978); Richard E. Neustadt and Harvey V. Fineberg, *The Swine Flu Affair* (Washington, D.C.: Government Printing Office, 1978); and Eugene Bardach and Robert Kagan, *Going by the Book* (Philadelphia: Temple University Press, 1982).

cess is less public than enactment politics, and the pattern of policy may be detectable only by paying attention to the repetition of minute details. We have learned enough of the politics of administration, however, to know that it does differ in important ways from enactment politics: interest groups, congressional committees, bureau chiefs, lesser officials, and the President are differently involved, play different roles, and have different resources and vastly different prospects of success in the different processes.

Less work has been done on a third process. This entails tracing the sources of public policies before they enter the highly focused arena of the enactment stage. It involves the politics of inventing, winnowing, and finding and gaining adherents for policy alternatives before they are made a part of a "program," and likewise the politics of moving alternatives from unlikely to possible to probable candidates for inclusion on an agenda for enactment.

We are not in total ignorance of the origins and background of a good many significant public policies. However, this knowledge has, on the whole, not been incorporated into general statements about the policymaking process. That this is the case can be illustrated by sampling a few general statements about policy initiation in America. These reflect not only commonly prevailing opinion, but well informed scholarly judgment as to the sources of public policy.

For example, in an especially thoughtful and rigorous presentation, Charles E. Lindblom discusses how congressmen

> depend upon "central" executive leadership, especially in the initiation of policies . . . e.g., in the degree to which the President has taken over the task of designing a legislative program for each succeeding Congress. . . . Congressional committees themselves, the chairmen themselves, have turned to the President for leadership in policymaking. . . . Perhaps 80 percent of bills enacted into law originate in the executive branch.[3]

In much the same vein James A. Robinson says,

> Congress' influence in foreign policy is primarily (and increasingly) to legitimate and/or amend recommendations initiated by the executive to

3. Charles E. Lindblom, *The Policy-Making Process* (Englewood Cliffs, N.J.: Prentice-Hall, 1968), p. 86. In the 1980 edition of this book, Lindblom modifies his view very slightly (pp. 60–61).

deal with situations usually identified by the executive. . . . Parliaments, Congresses and legislatures react to executive initiative rather than take initiative.[4]

This observation is supported by a chapter describing twenty-two foreign policy decisions from the 1930s to 1961, accompanied by a table listing the executive branch as the "initiator" in nineteen cases.[5] David B. Truman says:

The twentieth century, it is often noted, has been hard on legislatures. Compelled in some fashion to deal with the complexities of increasingly urbanized, rapidly industrialized, and irrevocably interdependent societies, they have found themselves alternating in varying degrees between two equally dangerous and distasteful situations, yielding the initiative as well as the implementing responsibilities to bureaucrats whose actions might be imperfectly mediated by political officials, or attempting to retain one or both of these functions at the expense of delay, indecision and instability.[6]

Samuel P. Huntington echoes the same theme: "The Congressional role in legislation has largely been reduced to delay and amendment."[7] He quotes a senator:

Congress has surrendered its rightful place of leadership in the lawmaking process to the White House. No longer is Congress the source of major legislation. It now merely filters legislative proposals from the President, straining out some and reluctantly letting others pass through. These days no one expects Congress to devise the important bills.[8]

He quotes a report of a congressional committee:

More and more the role of Congress has come to be that of a sometimes querulous but essentially kindly uncle who complains while furiously

4. James A. Robinson, *Congress and Foreign Policy Making*, 2d ed. (Evanston, Ill.: Dorsey Press, 1967), p. vii.

5. Ibid., pp. 23–69. This tabulation is heavily relied on by Aaron Wildavsky, who makes much the same point in "The Two Presidencies," *Trans-action* 4 (December 1967): 7–14.

6. David B. Truman, ed., *The Congress and America's Future* (Englewood Cliffs, N.J.: Prentice-Hall, 1965), pp. 1–2.

7. Samuel P. Huntington, "Congressional Responses to the 20th Century," ibid., pp. 5–31.

8. Ibid., p. 23.

puffing on his pipe but who finally, as everyone expects, gives in and hands over the allowance, grants one permission, or raises his hand in blessing, and then returns to the rocking chair for another year of somnolence.[9]

I wonder if this picture is not overdrawn. The evidence upon which remarks such as these are based attests to the following: immediately preceding the enactment of most laws, the agenda of Congress has frequently been addressed to proposals brought to it by the executive branch. Further, the resources of the executive branch have been focused upon the enactment of these proposals. This focusing process rests discretionarily and principally in the hands of modern American Presidents. Thus when the President adopts a proposal as part of his legislative program, when the President sends a bill to Capitol Hill, the President mobilizes resources behind a particular policy alternative, choosing one and excluding others. Through the power and the authority of his office he makes a strong and often successful claim on the attention of Congress. Thus, more than any other single actor, he can harness political energy and focus the political process in a meaningful and consequential way. But is he initiating policy? The conventional view is that he is.[10]

Yet no sophisticated student of contemporary American policy-making believes that policies normally spring fully formed from the overtaxed brow of the President or even from his immediate entourage.[11] Nor does policy appear out of the sea like Botticelli's Venus—dimpled, rosy, and complete on a clamshell. Where, then, and how are policies initiated in American politics?

---

9. Ibid., p. 24.

10. Among those taking a contrary view one might include John R. Johannes, *Policy Innovation in Congress* (Morristown, N.J.: General Learning Press, 1972), and Ronald Moe and Steven Teel, "Congress as Policy-Maker," *Political Science Quarterly* 85 (September 1970): 443–470. For a scrupulous and thorough review of the various positions see James L. Sundquist, *The Decline and Resurgence of Congress* (Washington, D.C.: Brookings Institution, 1981), pp. 148–154.

11. An excellent discussion of the presidential entourage in policymaking is contained in Alfred DeGrazia, *Republic in Crisis: Congress against the Executive Force* (New York: Federal Legal Publications, 1965), pp. 69–75.

2. METHODS: LIMITS AND OPPORTUNITIES

Obviously, the question has to be studied empirically.[12] Since a principal goal of the social scientific enterprise is to arrive at theories to which known levels of veracity may be ascribed, an important method of empirical demonstration entails carefully sampling from well-circumscribed populations. By drawing a sample at random from an entire population, it is possible to reach conclusions about the frequency with which various phenomena occur in the population and about events associated with occurrence and nonoccurrence. Thus we are led to plausible statements about causation.

This constitutes a powerful incentive to reject more casual methods of data collection. Sampling as the method of choice in empirical demonstration, however, in turn rests upon at least two conditions not presently met by the study of policy initiation. Sampling cannot take place at all without widespread agreement on the metes and bounds of the universe or population to be sampled. And it is wasteful to sample until the main outlines of what it is that will be empirically demonstrated are sufficiently clear. This is the dual rationale for the employment of case studies in the present essay. Case studies are a practical halfway house between arrant speculation and arid precision. On the one hand they provide empirical constraints that can guide speculation away from the embroidery of the genuinely idiosyncratic; on the other they can stimulate the production of ideas about how things are actually connected in the real world as a preliminary to more rigorous empirical demonstration. So long as our stock of ideas about policy initiation is relatively primitive, and so long as we are still learning and disagreeing about what a policy is and what an initiation is, the strategy of laying out case studies and searching for ideas about the experience they embody seems not only defensible but desirable.[13]

12. At the conclusion of their largely deductive chapter on planning and innovation in *Organizations* (New York: Wiley, 1958), James G. March and Herbert A. Simon emphatically agree, saying, "[E]mpirical evidence of a reliable and persuasive kind is almost nonexistent—a complaint we have made throughout this volume, but which applies with special force to the topic of [organizational] cognition" (p. 210).

13. Harry Eckstein makes an even stronger argument for the use of case studies—indeed stronger than is necessary for present purposes. See "Case Study and Theory in Political Science," in Fred I. Greenstein and Nelson W. Polsby, eds., *Handbook of Political Science* 7 (Reading, Mass.: Addison-Wesley, 1975), pp. 79–137.

There is in fact bound to be ambiguity about precisely what counts as a policy and a fortiori what counts as an innovation. I do not see any clear way through this methodological and ultimately, I suppose, theoretical thicket. There is so far as I know no standard that presently commands universal acceptance by which policies can be distinguished from nonpolicies or innovations from noninnovations.[14] Nor is there an accepted method to gauge with precision the magnitude of a policy or an innovation. Thus there seems to be no entirely fastidious way to circumscribe a population from which a meaningful sample of policy innovations can be drawn for inspection.[15] This annoying situation need not balk empirical inquiry on the subject of policy innovation in American politics. So long as general statements such as I have quoted, purporting to have empirical reference, are made, even clumsy efforts are in order to marshal evidence about them.

That is the purpose of the case studies that follow. In capsule form, they recite some of the circumstances surrounding the emergence of eight new policies in recent American political history. In some cases the innovation at the focus of a report resides in the creation of a new governmental agency that subsequently can be seen to enlarge or materially to affect the repertoire of responses the government makes to a given range of social problems. In other cases, the innovation consists of a policy or a set of policies that seem to have altered (or

14. If a policy is, for example, defined as a course of action or a set of decisions leading to a particular course of action, how consistent do the decisions have to be? How steadfastly unilinear the course? How proximate the decisions to the course of action?

15. At least two attempts at surveying a large population of innovations have been made, however: Grover Starling, "Innovation, Productivity and Public Policy" (University of Houston at Clear Lake, Houston, Tex., 1973, Mimeographed); and Jack Walker, "The Diffusion of Innovations in American States," *American Political Science Review* 63 (September 1969): 880–899. An interesting preliminary investigation of a somewhat different sort is Giandomenico Majone, "Policies as Theories" (Paper presented at the ECPR Workshop on Political Rationality, Louvain, Belgium, April 1976). See also William Solesbury's cross-national effort, which controls for subject matter: Solesbury, "Issues and Innovations in Environmental Policy in Britain, West Germany, and California," *Policy Analysis* 2 (Winter 1976): 1–38; William B. Gwyn, *Ombudsman Policy Innovation in the English-Speaking World* (Berkeley: Institute of Governmental Studies, 1980); and Clement E. Vose on twentieth-century attempts to amend the United States Constitution, in *Constitutional Change* (Lexington, Mass.: Lexington Books, 1972).

promise to alter) the lives of persons affected by them in substantial and fairly permanent ways.

Thus the "sample" of policies I shall consider have three character-istics in common: (1) they are relatively large-scale phenomena, highly visible to political actors and observers; (2) they embody from at least one point of view a break with preceding governmental responses to the range of problems to which they are addressed; and (3) unlike major "crises," with which they share the preceding traits, "innovations" have institutional or societal effects that are in a sense "lasting." No doubt the men who stood eyeball to eyeball with Khrushchev in the Cuban missile crisis received lasting lessons from the experience, but unless these lessons are in some way given institutional form, it is hard to see how even such a dramatic event could be classed as a policy innovation, however momentous its immediate consequences and even though it occasioned a temporary break with past policies and past methods of making policy.[16]

The case studies that follow are written from already published sources and do not embody any new findings of fact. If there is anything new about these accounts, it is the perspective from which they are told—the fact that numerous individual case studies are being viewed from the standpoint of what they can tell us about policy initiation in the political system in which they all occur.

Because the perspective taken here is usually a little different from those employed by the various authors of the materials on which I base my discussions, facts may from time to time take on emphases in my retelling different from the way they appeared in the original accounts. This may be regarded as pulling events out of shape in order to make a point, but my view is that events do not have intrinsic shapes, except in a trivial sense, and that the original arrangement of them probably does about as much violence to their intrinsic order-

16. The missile crisis was highly visible and of course entailed extraordinary effort on the part of major participants in American decision-making, but the central admin-istrative instrument of decision-making—the high level task force—saw frequent use in the Kennedy administration. See Elie Abel, *The Missile Crisis* (Philadelphia: Lippincott, 1966), and Robert F. Kennedy, *Thirteen Days: A Memoir of the Cuban Missile Crisis* (New York: Norton, 1969), and compare descriptions of Kennedy routine such as Richard F. Fenno, Jr., "The Cabinet: Index to the Kennedy Way," *New York Times Magazine*, April 22, 1962.

ing as a subsequent retelling with a different purpose or audience in mind. This "Rashomon Problem"—where everybody has a more or less coherent, but slightly different, version of the same sequence of events—is a fascinating one and is widely to be encountered in nonexperimental social research. Of course it extends far beyond the difficulty embodied in the film *Rashomon*, of reconciling differing accounts of the same event told by participants powerfully driven to self-justification. I shall not discuss the matter in further detail but signal the reader that such a problem exists in principle.[17]

In practice, it does not seem to me that the recounting of cases here departs significantly from what any other person is likely to make of the materials at hand. There exists the possibility that not all the information worth knowing about policy initiation in these cases was available to the authors of the case material upon which we relied. Because the demands I make upon these materials are fairly light, because the cases are illustrative and not conclusive, because I draw upon them to suggest hypotheses rather than to embalm conclusions, the possibility that new circumstantial material on one or more of them may someday come to light is not fatal to my enterprise.

The cases, it will be observed, fall within a relatively narrow time span. This was dictated by two considerations. They had to be recent enough to provide plausible information about contemporary patterns of policy innovation. They had to be old enough to have evoked a reasonably authoritative set of memoirs, narrative accounts, or descriptions, so that we could rely upon the availability of accurate raw materials. These two constraints drew us toward the period immediately following World War II. Although not all our cases are of this vintage, owing to our occasional good fortune in uncovering usable descriptive materials about more recent innovations, the post–World War II period has receded sufficiently to yield a good crop of memoirs and narrative accounts, and we can be reasonably sure that initiations of that period still visible to us today have some considerable claim on the designation "policy innovation."

Each of the cases recounts an accomplishment usually embodying a legislative victory from the standpoint of liberal Democrats of the

17. See the general discussion of the problem of the narrator's perspective in case studies by Harold Stein in the introduction to *Public Administration and Policy Development* (New York: Harcourt, Brace, 1952).

post—New Deal era. This should be seen as an artifact of the evidently inescapable historical context within which our work took
place rather than a statement of authorial preferences—even though
I might well have been rooting for the winning side in each case had I
been old enough or attentive enough to care. During the era from
which our cases are drawn, liberals were doing most of the initiating,
and conservatives were, on the whole, resisting. Would innovation
processes similar to those I shall be discussing be similarly engaged if
the policies to be examined were aimed at reducing rather than
increasing the repertoire of governmental responses? If the case
studies were of budgetary reconciliation or the new federalism, or of
an amendment to the Constitution putting limits on federal spending, would the conclusions be the same? Of course without doing the
work nobody can be certain of the answer, but I see no reason in
principle to believe that the natural history of political innovation
differs according to something as ephemeral as whose ox is gored or
whose position is sustained in the process. Readers should be alert,
however, to the possibility that this is an incorrect guess.

There are, so it seems, periods of expansion and periods of retrenchment in public-sector activity; in both, we can assume, epi-
sodes of political innovation can occur. Thus there is no reason to
assume a priori that processes which established graduated taxes
would be uninteresting to those who wish to establish the flat rate
income tax.

I must mention a final set of methodological—and substantive—
limitations of this study. Like the general statements about American
policymaking quoted above, the cases to be considered here all come
from a severely restricted domain, since all had a highly visible and
discrete enactment phase engaging the President and Congress. This
artificial limitation has weaknesses:

1. It overrepresents the products of "events" or "happenings." Anal-
   ogous to the journalist's enslavement to "news pegs,"[18] there is a
   systematic underrepresentation of innovations that build slowly,
   that accrete, for example, within the common law of administrative agencies.

18. See Bernard Cohen's perceptive discussion of this problem in journalism, in
Cohen, *The Press and Foreign Policy* (Princeton, N.J.: Princeton University Press,
1963), pp. 91—92.

2. It artificially restricts the consideration of innovations to those kinds characteristically processed within the arenas chosen as vantage points. It neglects innovation, for example, by state and city governments, by courts, and in the private sector.[19]

3. It classes as policy initiations those events that actually occurred and takes no account, even as a control, of those dozens or hundreds of nonevents which might have happened but did not.[20] This is an important limitation on the generality of statements that we might otherwise want to make in that the systematic study of processes that prevent innovative action—a study not undertaken here—can help to identify constraints applying to the domain within which innovations characteristically occur and hence to the range of applicability of findings about successful strategies of innovation.

19. These are hard to study, and not many scholars have tried. Yet there is no doubt that political innovations take place within these diverse arenas. See Wallace S. Sayre and Nelson W. Polsby, "American Political Science and the Study of Urbanization," in Leo Schnore and Philip Hauser, eds., *The Study of Urbanization* (New York: Wiley, 1965), pp. 115–156, especially pp. 142–143; Robert A. Dahl, "Business and Politics: A Critical Appraisal of Political Science," in Robert A. Dahl, Mason Haire, and Paul F. Lazarsfeld, *Social Science Research on Business: Product and Potential* (New York: Columbia University Press, 1959), pp. 3–43; Alfred D. Chandler, Jr., *Strategy and Structure* (Cambridge: MIT Press, 1962); Chandler, *The Visible Hand: The Managerial Revolution in American Business* (Cambridge: Harvard University Press, 1977); Lawrence B. Mohr, "Determinants of Innovation in Organizations," *American Political Science Review* 63 (March 1969): 111–126; Joel B. Grossman, "The Supreme Court and Social Change," *American Behavioral Scientist* 13 (March–April 1970): 535–551; and Walker, "Diffusion of Innovations in American States." See also Everett Rogers, *Diffusion of Innovations* (New York: Free Press of Glencoe, 1962), a review of more than five hundred publications on the diffusion of mostly technological innovations, and its second, expanded edition, *Communication of Innovations* by Rogers with F. Floyd Shoemaker (New York: Free Press, 1971). Literature on organizational innovations is summarized in Gerald Zaltman, Robert Duncan, and Jonny Holbeck, *Innovations and Organizations* (New York: Wiley, 1973).

20. This is an allusion to the famous problem of nondecisions, which receives its most extensive consideration in the literature of community power. See Peter Bachrach and Morton Baratz, "Two Faces of Power," *American Political Science Review* 56 (December 1962): 947–952; Matthew Crenson, *The Unpolitics of Air Pollution* (Baltimore: The Johns Hopkins University Press, 1971); and, for further discussion, Nelson W. Polsby, *Community Power and Political Theory: A Further Look at Problems of Evidence and Inference* (New Haven: Yale University Press, 1980), pp. 189–218.

It is a fact that some conceivable innovations do not occur, and some innovations that are possible in some political systems are not even conceivable in others. In part this is no doubt a product of the ambient values of a political culture. As we look around the world, we can easily see forms of social organization and political behavior uncongenial to American norms: regulations pertaining to family life, for example, or limitations on freedom of physical movement. We do not carry internal passports as some Europeans and the South Africans do. We do not—on the whole—rear our children apart from their parents, as the upper-class English and the Israeli kibbutzniks sometimes do. Our limitations on marriage and childbearing are generally far less stringent than can be found among the mainland Chinese. And, as so many commentators have noted, we have no large, activist socialist labor party bringing government ownership to various sectors of the economy and not much popular sentiment regretting this oversight.

While it is surely worthy of a scholar's attention to ask why none of these policies or conditions prevails in the United States, such a question constitutes a dubious strategy for discovering why we get the policy innovations we have. For even within the values of the American political culture, the technological capabilities of the society and its pattern of resource mobilization, and its characteristic mode of social organization, choices are made and alternatives considered, initiatives are taken and innovations emerge. For our purposes, the question is how.

There are undoubtedly other unmentioned problems, equally serious, which conceivably undermine a priori the generality one may claim for conclusions reached by careful study of the population of cases to be considered here. This is a fatal handicap, however, only to those who feel ready to pronounce with finality upon the problem at hand. The present essay is exploratory in character, and the restriction of coverage serves the function of providing a few crude controls so as to assure some sort of comparability between cases. Thus, while our method forbids the formulation of universals worthy of a high degree of confidence, it does facilitate the discovery of a few low- and middle-range generalizations.

Throughout the discussion that follows, I will use "policy initiation" and "innovation" more or less interchangeably although I can conceive of circumstances under which this usage might cause confusion. For my purposes, however, if a policy is not in some sense an innovation for the American system, the point at which it is adopted is not an initiation. Rather its initiation comes further back in time, when the policy is first introduced, and hence is an innovation.[21]

Thus, if it isn't an innovation, it isn't an initiation. In retrospect, at least, it is possible to discern what constitutes an important mutation in policy, and in reconstructing how these come about we discover policy initiations. Such initiations, of course, are different from the day-to-day initiatives that serve to activate the routines of government.

Some may wish to argue that there is no such thing as policy innovation in American politics, that even for our purposes, as for those of the Speaker in the book of Ecclesiastes, there is nothing new under the sun.[22] For such observers, a search for the genesis of policy innovations is bound to prove fruitless, since it is so difficult to settle definitively on the exact point in time at which any particular innovation emerged from the primordial ooze. An opinion of this sort cannot be met wholly on empirical grounds, because those who so argue may be unwilling to stipulate any conditions under which a search for beginnings may be regarded as successfully completed.

Those who are more curious about the shape of the real world, however, may be willing to accept some necessary compromises. To them I propose the three criteria of large scale and visibility, break with preceding habit, and lasting consequences. These criteria are not only serviceable for guiding the selection of case materials to be presented here, but also can be used to marshal further evidence that can qualify or weaken general statements I shall offer in passing and in conclusion. It is my hope that they will be acceptable, for it is by such convoluted means—and I fear perhaps only by such means—that a generalized description of processes of policy initiation in such a complex environment as the American political system can in time be given appropriate empirical foundations.

21. This usage comports with that employed by James G. March and Herbert A. Simon in *Organizations*, pp. 174ff. Their definition: "Initiation and innovation are present when change requires the devising and evaluation of new performance programs that have not been a part of the organization's repertory and cannot be introduced by a simple application of programmed switching rules" (pp. 174–175).

22. Eccles. 1:9.

3. A BRIEF GUIDE TO THE CASES

While, as I suppose, there is no good substitute for immersion in the messy facts of the empirical world if we are to give some sort of realistic basis to a study of the politics of innovation, the problem still remains that the facts are in some instances extraordinarily messy. Total immersion can lead to waterlogging, if not drowning. Thus it has seemed sensible to take a few preliminary steps toward sorting out elementary dimensions that could guide the reading—as in time they did the writing—of the case materials.

Essentially I sought descriptive dimensions through which I could expound a plausible natural history of political innovations in a number of different real-world settings and circumstances. I expected cases to vary with respect to these dimensions, but also that the dimensions would prove to be useful—as indeed in most instances they were—in recording general observations applicable to more than one case. They are:

1. Timing: Elapsed time between first proposal and enactment. Some innovations move swiftly into the enactment phase; others take years.
2. Specialization: Restriction of policy formation to specialists versus early and significant participation in the shaping of alternatives by political generalists. The distinction here is between "experts" and "politicians" as sources of policy alternatives.
3. Existence of agreement in the decision-making subculture: Some policies hatch in an atmosphere in which there is strong agreement that a "need" exists. Others are at first not unanimously regarded as problematic by officials. Members of a decision-making group may or may not agree on solutions and may or may not agree about what the problems are. When agreement about the character of problems is missing, decision-makers have not developed a subculture in which they are sharing norms and expectations about policy initiation.
4. Public Saliency: Some innovations receive little attention and support in public arenas, others a great deal, before they enter the phase of enactment.
5. Political Conflict: Some innovations generate little public or political opposition, others a great deal.

6. Research: Some innovations are improvised; for others questions of technical design explicitly arise and are the product of the application of much sophisticated effort, and empirical premises of innovations are systematically examined.
7. Staging: Separation versus temporal juxtaposition or fusion of the processes of invention and search. For some innovations, alternatives are proposed well before the need for a solution is widely recognized; for others, the recognition of the need and the invention of a solution occur together, or, in the apt jargon of modern organization theory, solutions chase problems rather than problems seeking solutions.[23]

These are some of the considerations I shall be bearing in mind as I address the case materials and undertake to compare and contrast specific instances of policy innovation.

23. See Michael D. Cohen, James G. March, and Johan P. Olsen, "A Garbage Can Model of Organizational Choice," *Administrative Science Quarterly* 17 (March 1972), who describe situations in which "an organization is a collection of choices looking for problems, issues and feelings looking for decision situations in which they might be aired, solutions looking for issues to which they might be the answer, and decision makers looking for work" (p. 2).

II

Postwar Science Policy: Three Innovations

Policy innovations generally follow upon the identification of a need. Needs are in a sense ubiquitous: everybody needs something, as the songwriters almost put it. So along with a simple state of tension somewhere in society there also must exist a doctrine, or theory, or idea, or notion, or attitude, or custom, that legitimizes governmental activity with respect to this need. It follows from this that it ought to be relatively easy to innovate with respect to needs created by organizational opportunities or custodial difficulties within public bureaucracies, since the innovation can be rationalized as necessary to the pursuit of goals already sanctioned by the existence of machinery. Among our cases of innovation in science policy are illustrations of this point.

The generation of scientists who began their work before World War II occasionally waxes nostalgic about the era before scientific activity became a major concern of the United States government.[1] But even before the United States entered the war, that era had drawn to a close. The critical events that form a part of the backdrop for the vast increase in governmental interest in science are well

---

1. Daniel Lang reports: "Before the war, . . . physicists were a poor but happy lot. There were relatively few of them, and they kept pretty much to themselves. Those were . . . 'the string-and-sealing-wax days'—an allusion to the makeshift materials with which physicists often put their rudimentary apparatus together in cramped laboratories somewhere out behind the gym on this or that university campus. Nowadays, both government and industry are pumping billions of dollars into this once impoverished profession." He quotes the physicist Samuel Goudsmit:
It's been a shock. . . . We've got marvelous laboratories for basic research, which is the real love of any self-respecting physicist, but somehow we don't have the same tender affection for them that we would have had years ago, when acquiring a three-hundred-dollar spectroscope was reason enough for throwing a party.

known: the scientific discovery that certain very heavy atoms could be made to release enormous amounts of energy, the apprehension in the scientific community that this knowledge was available to scientists in the Third Reich, the maneuvers by prominent scientists in the United States to inform President Roosevelt, the decision by Roosevelt to mobilize American science through a science advisory committee, the formation of the Manhattan Project, and so on.

Once the war was well on the way to being won, a new set of problems naturally arose with respect to the continuing relations between science and government. To what extent would government continue to pay for the development of science? Who would set the priorities for scientific effort? How would the technologies that wartime science had created be managed and controlled? Questions such as these forced themselves upon the attention of scientists and political leaders as World War II drew to a close. In some respects the problems they posed were unprecedented. Other heavily mobilized parts of the economy could with more or less dislocation be demilitarized and remilitarized as needed: manpower, steel production,

---

Today we're given a multi-million-dollar piece of equipment, and the minute the dedication ceremonies are over, we're poring over plans for an even more powerful one. In the old days physicists gave themselves up wholly to a single-minded study of the fundamental laws of the universe. Now we feel called upon to do things of a sort we never even imagined we'd be doing—thoroughly unscientific things. We sit down with the Defense Secretary to help him figure out his next year's budget. We brief the President of the United States on the nation's nuclear stockpile. We're at Eniwetok or Las Vegas, or we're talking with troop commanders in Europe or Japan. We teach physics to Navy officers who are going to run nuclear-powered submarines. Air Force generals used to be just newsreel figures to us, but now they're fellows we have to talk over atomic-driven planes and plan offensive and defensive tactics with. Some of us are in industry, designing electronic equipment, and some of us are attached to the American embassy staffs in England, France, and Germany. Colleagues of mine who never even bothered to vote before Hiroshima now sit at the elbows of our United Nations representatives when the subject of atomic energy is on the agenda. And others, who were ill at ease lecturing before a few seminar students, now address large audiences on the fate that threatens the world if atomic energy is not internationally controlled. From timid pedagogue to eloquent Jeremiah—all in the space of a few short years.

Daniel Lang, *The Man in the Thick Lead Suit* (New York: Oxford University Press, 1954), pp. 150–151. See also Laura Fermi, *Atoms in the Family* (Chicago: University of Chicago Press, 1954).

fabricating plants, and so on. Factories—indeed, entire cities—constructed for the purpose of making components for atomic bombs seemed on the face of it less amenable to easy conversion to the private sector. The stake that government now had in the skills and activities of the scientific community was far different from that of the days before the war—and this difference did not apply in the same measure to any other comparable group in the working population. Finally, there was the acute problem of the drastic change that science had wrought in the world balance of power.

Three postwar policy innovations (among others) addressed these problems: the proposal to establish civilian control of atomic energy, the establishment of the National Science Foundation (NSF), and the proposal of a nuclear test ban treaty. Because at the time each of these innovations was proposed most large-scale science was carried on under government auspices, the identification of the need, the search for solutions, and the generation and proposal of options took place almost exclusively within the government itself.

1. CIVILIAN CONTROL OF ATOMIC ENERGY

There is a view implicit in the selection of any issue for separate attention that it has large intrinsic significance. Therefore it is important to stress at the outset that civilian control of atomic energy does not seem to have been so regarded by the main actors present at the creation of the postwar Atomic Energy Commission (AEC). Far from being the central conception that animated the debate over the Commission's formation, the principle of civilian control emerged very late in a complicated process of deliberation.[2]

As the war's end approached, major questions arose concerning the future development of wartime scientific discoveries and the roles to be assumed in this development by the government, the

2. The principal source for this case is a study having official sanction: Richard G. Hewlett and Oscar E. Anderson, Jr., *The New World, 1939–1946: A History of the Atomic Energy Commission* 1 (University Park, Pa.: Pennsylvania State University Press, 1962). I have relied heavily on this study throughout. See also A. Hunter Dupree, *Science in the Federal Government* (Cambridge: Harvard University Press, 1957); and Alice K. Smith, *A Peril and a Hope* (Chicago: University of Chicago Press, 1965).

military, and civilian scientists. Because their direct participation in the creation of atomic power left many scientists particularly sensitive to the need for international control and to the potentialities for domestic use, and because their extensive involvement in wartime governmental research gave them a clear stake in postwar governmental research policy, it was scientists who as often as not began raising these questions in semipublic ways.

By the fall of 1943, the scientists based at the Metallurgical Laboratory at the University of Chicago were aware that their assignment to produce plutonium was nearing an end, and rumors abounded locally that 90 percent of the personnel there would be released by mid-1944. To quell the rumors, and to provide directions for postwar research (and thus maintain the project staff intact), laboratory director Arthur H. Compton commissioned a staff report on future research goals. The report, arguing that these goals should be broadened to incorporate examination of nonmilitary applications of nuclear energy and support of continued basic research, was presented in April 1944 to General Leslie Groves, head of the Manhattan Engineering District and administrator of the Military Policy Committee, which was charged with overall coordination of atomic military development.[3] Groves failed to see the need for postwar planning at this point, however, and proposed a large reduction in staff for the Chicago project.

In order to avoid this retrenchment, Compton appointed a second committee to prepare detailed technical proposals for atomic research; at Compton's urging, wartime overall science czar Vannevar Bush appointed his own committee to do the same. Compton's committee interpreted its mandate broadly and, among its more concrete proposals aimed at continuing work for existing government-sponsored scientific groups, recommended a United States–initiated international atomic energy control organization. The Bush committee confined itself to recommending a national science agency to "distribute funds among military and civilian laboratories of the government, academic institutions, and industrial organizations."

3. Two other members of the Committee were chairman Vannevar Bush, President of the Carnegie Institution and wartime governmental czar of scientific activities, and James B. Conant, a distinguished chemist and President of Harvard. Hewlett and Anderson, *New World*, p. 83.

The official historians of the Atomic Energy Commission comment:

> The . . . reports had two things in common: first, they called for national support of a comprehensive nuclear energy program after the war; second, they had no immediate impact. This does not mean that the Army shoved them into pigeonholes and promptly forgot about them. Bush and [his deputy, James B.] Conant were alert to the need for planning. They knew the value of scientific research. They did not need reports to tell them it was crucial to devise effective arrangements for national and international control. . . . Until they could interest the officials who had to make these essentially political decisions, the . . . analysis of the working scientists had little utility.[4]

In July 1944 Bush and Conant asked Irwin Stewart, a member of the Military Policy Committee staff, to draw up a bill for submission to Congress on postwar control of atomic energy. The draft bill provided for a commission that would engage private contractors to construct production plants, operate all atomic-powered facilities, and conduct all nuclear experiments involving any amount of fissionable material. Bush and Conant consciously designed the twelve-member commission to be free of "political pressures": five nominees from the National Academy of Science, three part-time civilian members appointed by the President, and four members divided equally between the Army and the Navy Departments. All members were to serve fixed and staggered five-year terms.

Bush and Conant attempted to solicit support in the administration for their draft bill by urging the need for orderly development of nuclear power on Secretary of War Henry Stimson. They argued that since the United States and Britain could not maintain a monopoly on the bomb, a disastrous arms race could only be prevented by making all technical details of the atomic bomb and any other nuclear scientific information public through an international agency. Bush also discussed postwar scientific planning at length with President Roosevelt, but the emphasis in this discussion was on international control, a policy that would have to be negotiated with the other major powers.

The Bush and Conant efforts were rewarded when Stimson agreed to the idea of an advisory commission on atomic energy control.

4. Hewlett and Anderson, *New World*, p. 325.

Stimson, in turn, in late April 1945, advised newly installed President Truman of the scientific community's concerns. In early May, Stimson recommended to Truman that the latter establish an "Interim Committee" to advise on postwar atomic policy and that the Committee include Stimson, Bush, Conant, and Stimson's special consultant George L. Harrison, President of the New York Life Insurance Company. Truman approved both the idea of a committee and the proposed membership.

By the Committee's first meeting, in May of 1945, the war in Europe had ended, and Committee members felt sure that domestic and international control and development of atomic energy would soon become major public issues. International control was felt to depend on the outcome of Three-Power talks, and thus to be outside the immediate province of Committee action, but domestic control might well be influenced by the first governmental group to recommend specific action on it. In anticipation of this, alternate chairman Harrison had recruited two War Department lawyers, General Kenneth Royall (later Secretary of the Army) and William Marbury, to draft a proposal on postwar domestic control of atomic energy for the Committee to consider at its first meeting.

The Royall-Marbury proposal was very similar to the Bush-Conant "bill" of the previous year in several ways.

1. Scope. Complete custody of all raw materials, plant facilities, technical information and patents, contracts for production, and all atomic research was to be in the hands of the new agency.
2. Form of organization. A commission was again proposed, insulated from "political pressure" by the President's limited power to remove commissioners and by the commission's ability to choose its own operating director.
3. Membership. Part-time commissioners were proposed, slightly more than half to be civilians, slightly fewer than half to be military appointees from the Departments of War and the Navy.

The Interim Committee did not immediately adopt the proposal, however, since both its original instigators, Bush and Conant, had changed their minds on many provisions. Royall felt that military representation was necessary to secure congressional support, but Conant and Bush no longer supported formal military representation; "civilian control" versus "military domination" (later "military representation") thus made its first appearance as an issue, but it was not a major bone of contention at this point. Bush was much more concerned with the scope of the organization. Specifically, he felt that commission control of research was far too great, arguing that there should be quantitative limits on materials, below which nonregulated research should be allowed, and that the commission should not contract for research at all, but merely regulate such work. Bush was then also engaged in planning legislation for a National Research Foundation (later the NSF), which would be an appropriate sponsor for such scientific research.

The original judgment that time was of the essence in forming the Committee and shaping plans for postwar atomic energy control proved to be correct. The bombing of Hiroshima on August 6, 1945, suddenly brought atomic energy to public attention, jolted several congressional committees into action, and threatened to bury Bush's objections to the Royall-Marbury plan, which had the overwhelming virtue of being available at a time when a "need" for public policy became acute.

In announcing that for the first time in history atomic weapons had been used, President Truman stated that he would immediately request legislation establishing a commission to control the production and use of atomic power. The bombing of Hiroshima placed immediate discussions of atomic energy in an international context, however; thus Truman's attention was first focused on developing a position for negotiations with the USSR and Great Britain, and his speech reconvening Congress on September 7 contained no mention of domestic control.

Secretary Stimson, who had been the major pipeline from the atomic energy establishment to Truman on domestic control matters, was taken ill at this point and was effectively out of action until his retirement in late September. In the absence of the Secretary of War, alternate chairman of the Interim Committee George Harrison pressed Undersecretary of State Dean Acheson to advocate an amended version of the Royall-Marbury bill to Congress, but Acheson demurred on the grounds that this would raise questions of international control on which the President was still undecided.

Lack of prompt action by the administration on domestic atomic energy control did not deter various senators and representatives from introducing bills in this area, and Acheson discovered while testifying before the Senate Foreign Relations Committee on September 19, 1945, that unless the administration threw its weight behind some specific proposals, growing committee jurisdictional disputes would stymie any legislation in the near future. At this hearing, Senator Arthur Vandenberg of Michigan, senior Republican on the Foreign Relations Committee, remarked that since no one committee had clear jurisdiction over what amounted to a new subject area, there would be a race among several committee chairmen to gain control by getting their pet bills reported.

Acheson's response was to assign an assistant, Herbert S. Marks, to draft a presidential message to Congress on both domestic and international aspects of atomic energy. Having read the Royall-Marbury draft, Marks incorporated their commission proposal into his message. While the message never unequivocally committed the President to this one plan, President Truman delivered essentially Marks's draft to Congress on October 3, thus giving an apparent presidential blessing to the Royall-Marbury "bill."

Secretary of War Patterson, a strong supporter of Royall-Marbury, was anxious to have the bill sent to the two Military Affairs Committees, with which his department had amicable relations, and the President's message provided the needed impetus for its introduction. The bill was trumpeted as "the President's wishes" because of its similarity to the Marks draft of his speech, but in fact it had never been cleared with the Bureau of the Budget or other executive agencies.[5] In the House, the plan was sponsored by Andrew May of Kentucky, chairman of the Military Affairs Committee, and in the Senate an identical bill was introduced by Edwin Johnson of Colorado, a senior Democratic majority member of the Senate counterpart committee. Senator Vandenberg, however, argued that this was not merely a military question, thereby inaugurating the promised jurisdictional battle:

> This is infinitely more than a military question. It is a question touching every phase of civilian life . . . fundamentally it is a question touching

5. A formal clearance process had been established for all bills that were part of "the President's program." See Richard E. Neustadt, "Presidency and Legislation: the Growth of Central Clearance," *American Political Science Review* 48 (September 1954): 641–671.

our international relations; and so far as the immediate problem is concerned, the international phase is even more important than the domestic phase. The Committee on Foreign Relations has had jurisdiction over the subject to as great an extent as has the Committee on Military Affairs. I know of no reason why this proposal should go to the Committee on Military Affairs.[6]

The Senate had already passed, five days before the President's speech, a Vandenberg resolution calling for a joint committee to deal with all atomic energy bills, and Vandenberg used the need to wait for House action on this resolution as a device to block assignment of the Johnson bill to any Senate committee.

Vandenberg's Senate maneuver did not stop action in the House, however. Chairman May held only one day of sympathetic hearings, on October 9, on the May (née Royall-Marbury) bill, a tactic that irritated many atomic scientists. Groups of scientists at Chicago and Oak Ridge warned publicly against hasty action on such legislation, and the noted Chicago scientist Leo Szilard denounced the bill. The scientists' main grievances were (1) omission of reference to peacetime uses, and of provisions to foster peaceful research and development; (2) the fact that agency powers to dismiss employees were absolute, with no possibility of appeal and no need to make the grounds public (abuses of this power were freely predicted, since those associated with the Manhattan Project felt that such abuses had been responsible for a postwar scientific exodus there); (3) the fact that research would be permitted only under licensing, which was in turn under full military control; and (4) excessive secrecy and compartmentalization, similar to that which had kept various wartime project scientists from communicating with each other.

From the standpoint of the May-Johnson bill's backers, . . . haste was well advised. No sooner was the bill introduced than there rose from atomic scientists throughout the nation an avalanche of outraged criticism that could only have been spontaneous and deeply felt. During the operations of the Manhattan Project in war time, there had gradually developed a cleavage between most scientists and their supervisors. This division occurred as well between the handful of administrator-scientists in key positions and their brethren in the various laboratories

6. October 3, 1945, *Congressional Record*, 79th Cong., 1st sess., 91, pt. 7:9323.

operated by the Project. The former group became increasingly divorced from the work and problems of the working scientists and more under the influence of the military leaders. At the war's end they had long since ceased to represent the viewpoint of most scientists. Without here repeating the many incidents which explain the unenthusiastic attitude of most scientists toward military supervision, it may be sufficient to cite the conclusion of one of the key men in the Project that the military "delayed the bomb by eighteen months."[7]

The surprisingly vigorous adverse reaction to his hasty hearings caused chairman May to hold an additional day of hearings for scientists to testify. The committee treated its additional witnesses with hostility and stood by provisions for stringent penalties for unauthorized disclosure of classified information. This by now was the major issue as far as the scientific community was concerned; unlike many politicians of that era, the scientists were convinced that it was impossible to keep scientific knowledge secret for any length of time. Opposition to the May-Johnson bill was important at this point in launching the Federation of Atomic Scientists, an organization having wide concerns with science, technology, and human affairs, and founded principally by Chicago scientists.

Whatever the motivation for May's speedy hearings—urgency of the national need for a bill, or urgency of the Committee's need to control any bill in the area—Senator Vandenberg realized that his joint committee proposal had been blocked in the House. He therefore came to the support of a substitute proposal by freshman Democratic Senator Brian McMahon of Connecticut to create a special Senate committee to examine the problems of atomic energy and all bills related to the subject. Majority Leader Alben Barkley had tried to send the Johnson bill to the Military Affairs Committee, but after two hours of debate he decided that Republican opposition, plus that of Democrats who were attracted by Vandenberg's argument that the Senate should not give in so freely to the President on this matter, plus the views of Democrats already opposed to the May-Johnson bill (such as members of the Foreign Relations Committee and a few

7. Byron S. Miller, "A Law Is Passed—The Atomic Energy Act Of 1946," *Chicago Law Review* 15 (Summer 1948): 804. Cf. Peter Michelmore, *The Swift Years: The Robert Oppenheimer Story* (New York: Dodd, Mead, 1969), p. 119.

others) would be enough to defeat the move, so he and the rest of the Senate acquiesced in the McMahon proposal.

The McMahon resolution establishing the special committee provided (as is the custom) that since there was at that point no Vice-President, the chairman should be chosen by the President Pro Tempore. This was the aged Kenneth McKellar of Tennessee, who would have preferred to let the entire Senate or the new committee appoint the chairman, since the task of doing so thrust him right back into a new form of the original jurisdictional dispute. McMahon pointed out that original sponsors of bills creating the last seventeen special committees had been made chairmen thereof. McKellar followed the precedent and appointed McMahon chairman, but, as is also quite usual, constituted the rest of the committee so as to smooth over the jurisdictional problem. All but one of the nonfreshman members were from the Military Affairs or Foreign Relations Committees. McMahon's inexperience as chairman was balanced by the appointment of veteran conservatives to the other seats on the committee. The Democratic members were all quite senior senators: Johnson of Colorado, of Military Affairs; Tom Connally of Texas, chairman of Foreign Relations; Millard E. Tydings of Maryland and Richard B. Russell of Georgia, both powerful members of Military Affairs; and Harry F. Byrd of Virginia, chairman of Naval Affairs. Republican members were Vandenberg, Eugene D. Millikin of Colorado, Bourke B. Hickenlooper of Iowa, and Thomas C. Hart, a retired admiral who had recently been appointed to the Senate as McMahon's junior colleague from Connecticut.

On October 31, four days after the McMahon Committee was named, the House Military Affairs Committee reported out the May bill. The uproar surrounding its hearings had alerted Speaker Rayburn to its controversiality. After conferring with President Truman (who had himself been alerted to the hearings by his normal congressional sources as well as by members of his staff—notably Office of War Mobilization and Reconversion [OWMR] lawyer James R. Newman), Rayburn and Rules Committee chairman Adolf Sabath agreed that the bill would not leave the House Rules Committee and be scheduled for floor debate until the new Senate committee had reported.

McMahon disliked the May-Johnson bill, but felt that he and his new committee were not knowledgeable enough to draft substitute legislation. To fill the knowledge gap, and to guarantee a draft bill that would be different from May-Johnson, McMahon persuaded James Newman to accept appointment as the Committee's special counsel. McMahon had heard that Newman did not favor the May-Johnson bill. He had been impressed by Newman's familiarity with the subject matter and by his ability to speak about it in terms comprehensible to the layman when the two men had met the previous summer at the home of California Representative Helen Gahagan Douglas.

A foretaste of what was to come from the committee staff was suggested by Newman's appointment of Dr. Edward U. Condon as the committee's technical specialist: Condon was one of the three scientists (Szilard and Harold Urey were the others) most active in whipping up scientific opposition to the May-Johnson bill during its "too hasty" hearings. Even aside from his extraordinary role in the creation of the postwar structure of governmental control over atomic energy, James Newman was by any standard a remarkable man.[8] Although trained as a lawyer, he was a devoted scientific hobbyist and outrider in the scientific community. He had collaborated on writings giving popular treatments of scientific matters and after the war edited the successful anthology *The World of Mathematics*.[9] He had also served in the War Department as assistant to Secretary Patterson.

During the fall of 1945, McMahon conducted hearings and took lengthy tours of atomic energy installations, in an attempt to give Newman time to develop an alternative bill. Newman's view of the May-Johnson bill was that (1) the proposed commission had far too wide a jurisdiction, (2) the administrator should not be independent of the President, (3) penalties and procedures for dismissal from commission employ were highly punitive and should be contingent

8. See Alfred Friendly, "Chain-Reacting Liberal," *New Republic* 114 (June 17, 1946): 867–868.

9. James R. Newman, ed., *The World of Mathematics* (New York: Simon and Schuster, 1956).

on court conviction, and (4) the commission's membership and scope tended to overemphasize military exploitation of atomic energy, to the detriment of peaceful uses. In mid-October Newman had passed on these qualms in a memo to his boss, OWMR Director John Snyder, who at the time was assistant president for domestic affairs, and Snyder in turn brought them to the attention of his close friend President Truman.[10]

Truman was intrigued and asked Snyder to summarize criticism of the May-Johnson bill. This request was bucked down to Newman, who reported the scientists' criticisms and pointed out to Truman that a major drawback of the bill was the administrator's independence of the President. After receiving Budget Bureau Director Harold Smith's separate but similar analysis several days later, Truman asked the OWMR to develop an administration policy and immediately informed Secretary of War Patterson that the May-Johnson bill did not represent the President's final view on the subject.

The May-Johnson bill emerged from the House Military Affairs Committee on November 5, but it was not until December 20 that Newman's proposals were ready for McMahon's special Senate committee. Newman was in a unique position. While working for the McMahon Committee he maintained his office in OWMR, with its relatively easy access to the President through Director Snyder. Thus a single staff person was in a position to influence decisively both the administration's position and the Senate bill and could draw upon considerable informal knowledge of both the military and the scientific communities.

Newman's proposal to the McMahon Committee called for a five-man commission of full-time members, appointed by the President, to serve at his pleasure. The commission would have four operating divisions, the directors of which would also be appointed by the President. The commission would own all patents relevant to production of fissionable material, but those concerned with peaceful uses would be available through nonexclusive licenses. Information flow was to be relatively unrestricted; the commission would play an

10. For a study of this special relationship, see Herman Miles Somers, *Presidential Agency: OWMR* (Cambridge: Harvard University Press, 1950), pp. 50–88.

active role in encouraging private research, and all activities using materials that were "non-fissionable" would be free of controls. This cut back the scope of the May-Johnson bill slightly. The commission's powers were circumscribed, the commission was placed squarely under the President's control, and the military was excluded from representation on the five-man commission.

A second series of hearings, this time before McMahon's Senate committee and on the McMahon (Newman) proposal, began on January 22, 1946. Secretary of the Navy James Forrestal and Secretary of War Patterson each argued that they were not opposed to civilian control, but only to military exclusion, and they proposed changes in the structure of the commission to make it more like an interlocking directorate of relevant cabinet-level officials. President Robert Hutchins of the University of Chicago and several scientist witnesses attempted to rebut this by depicting the Secretaries as favoring military dominance, but the senators on the committee who cross-examined them argued that the issue was military representation, not military control.

Newman alerted President Truman to the Secretaries' testimony and to committee sentiment, and on January 25 Truman sent Patterson a letter drafted by Newman, stating that (1) the commission "should be exclusively composed of civilians," (2) a governmental monopoly of possession and production of all fissionable materials was necessary, and (3) there should be access to atomic energy devices through private licensing—all provisions of the McMahon bill. Truman amplified his position by publicly endorsing Commerce Secretary Henry Wallace's testimony attacking the May-Johnson bill for its inclusion of the military on the commission, its lack of a statement on patents, and its weak presidential control of the commission. In the first week of February, Truman sent an open letter to McMahon (again drafted by Newman) congratulating him on his hearings, reiterating his previous three points, and adding that any bill should not stifle independent scientific research.

On February 14, Secretary Patterson testified again before the McMahon Committee. Three days before his appearance, he had submitted a War Department critique of the McMahon bill to the Budget Bureau for clearance; the critique had been routed to Newman at OWMR, who delayed clearance. Patterson did succeed in getting to see President Truman the night before his testimony and received permission to state his opposition to "military exclusion," but not to release his critique. Newman's (and Truman's) efforts to see that the military Secretaries did not express public opposition to the President's preferences were undone, however, as a result of the February 16 arrest of twenty-two persons in Ottawa for passing secret atomic energy information to the Soviets.

General Groves (of the Manhattan District) testified about these disclosures in a closed session of the McMahon Committee, and Committee members were enough impressed by his testimony to invite him back to comment publicly on the atomic energy legislation, despite the strenuous objections of McMahon. Speaking "for himself and not the War Department," Groves argued that the commission must contain men with military experience, or, failing that, that all its policy decisions should be required to be cleared with the Joint Chiefs of Staff—the latter being one of the major points in Patterson's suppressed War Department critique of the McMahon bill.

The attempts of the scientific community to downgrade the importance of "secrecy" were somewhat discredited by the Ottawa arrests, but the Federation of Atomic Scientists was galvanized into a massive letter-writing, public speaking, and advertising campaign by the acknowledgment in a short statement on the House floor on March 11 by Representative Andrew May that the War Department was helping him push his bill through the House. Media coverage and public interest were very intense as the Senate Special Committee began marking up atomic energy legislation. Senator Vandenberg, the ranking minority member, emerged as the de facto leader of the Committee, rather than chairman McMahon, who continually found himself outnumbered.

Vandenberg first proposed that all commission decisions relevant to military matters be subject to review by the Army Chief of Staff. Newman, through Snyder, wrote a memo alerting Truman to the change, and Snyder appended a suggestion that Truman discuss it with Army Chief of Staff Eisenhower. Eisenhower came out publicly against such military review, and the Committee settled for a military advisory board with which the commission would have to consult, and which would have the right to appeal all decisions related to national defense to the President. This amendment passed six to one,

McMahon opposing. Its passage brought immediate attacks on Vandenberg by Secretary Wallace, in a Chicago speech, and by various scientific organizations, through press releases. Vandenberg was infuriated, and called a special committee meeting at which he changed the advisory board's jurisdiction from "national defense" to all matters concerned with "common defense and security." The Federation of Atomic Scientists and its affiliated National Committee on Atomic Information resumed their campaign to arouse public opinion on "military dominance," and chairman McMahon himself asked over nationwide radio in a speech to the Overseas Press Club whether the nation wanted "military dominance or civilian development."

The Special Committee met on April 1, 1946, to go over a new draft developed by Newman and other Committee staff members, incorporating successive revisions of the Committee's March work. The new bill had a presidentially appointed five-man commission and a presidentially appointed general manager. There would be four operating divisions—research, production, engineering, and military applications—whose directors would be chosen by the commission. There was also to be a scientific advisory committee, a military liaison committee, and a congressional joint committee on atomic energy. Senator Vandenberg proposed that the military liaison committee be appointed by the service department secretaries rather than by the President, and that its jurisdiction revert from "common defense" to "military applications"; these provisions and the amended bill were passed without a dissenting vote. On June 1, the bill passed the Senate by voice vote.

There was some feeling on the House Military Affairs Committee that since they had reported a bill (the May bill) that had been "the President's desire" six months before, only to see their work preempted and attacked in the Senate, there was no particular hurry about considering this new proposal in the slightly over one month left before adjournment. On June 3, House Speaker Sam Rayburn, after conferring with President Truman, told May's committee that he and the President preferred the McMahon bill. May began hearings on June 10 with Secretary of War Patterson, who testified that the McMahon bill in fact protected national defense interests better than the earlier bill.

May announced his support for the Senate bill and his hope to have it reported at the end of the hearings (June 22), but a variety of delays stalled the bill for nearly a month. Several members of the Committee were ill or already home campaigning, and the most enthusiastic pro-McMahon member, Representative Chet Holifield (D-Calif.), was at the Bikini atomic tests. Nine Republican members of the Committee had originally filed a minority report denouncing the May-Johnson bill as "socialistic," and the McMahon bill was anathema to them. With several Democrats missing, and several others firmly committed to more, not less, military control, these Republicans were able continually to adjourn Committee sessions for lack of a quorum. May's wartime business transactions were at this time under scrutiny by the Senate special committee investigating the national defense program, an investigation which on columnist Drew Pearson's instigation was eventually to stir up enough adverse information to defeat May's reelection and ultimately to convict him for conspiracy to defraud the government. As that committee's investigation continued, May's apparent desire to report out the McMahon bill grew.

> Newman was convinced the bill was dead unless it could be blasted out of the committee. He urged the President to see Speaker Rayburn and ask him to contact each Democratic member personally. The members should attend the hearings or leave their proxies with Representative Thomason. Just how the job was done remained shadowed in mystery. Perhaps a sharp reminder from the Speaker was enough inducement for most of the faithful. For May, there may have been an added incentive. . . . The Mead committee was collecting records on the Garsson munitions enterprises and was preparing to open public hearings which would implicate the congressman. Whether or not May knew the committee had written evidence of his calls to the War Department on behalf of the Garsson interests, he must have suspected the worst. On July 2, the day his name was first involved in the open hearings of the Mead committee, May announced that the McMahon bill had been reported out by a vote of twenty-four to three.[11]

The Committee approved an amendment authorizing the armed

---

11. Hewlett and Anderson, *New World*, p. 520.

forces (rather than an atomic energy commission) to produce atomic weapons and added three other amendments designed to give the military a greater voice in commission affairs: (1) at least one, but no more than two, of the five commissioners should represent the military, (2) the director of the military applications division should be an active military officer, and (3) active military officers should be permitted to serve in any position on the commission's staff.

A surprise attempt by House Un-American Activities Committee (HUAC) and Rules Committee member J. Parnell Thomas (R-N.J.) to kill the bill in the Rules Committee—on the basis of a HUAC report that if scientists were given control of atomic energy, the national security would be in danger—very nearly succeeded, and the bill was narrowly reported out of the Rules Committee on July 13.

The bill nearly died again on the first floor vote, when Representative John Rankin's (D-Miss.) motion to strike the enabling clause failed by only nine votes. The opposition strategy then became to amend the bill so copiously that it would be unacceptable to the Senate, while the goal of Representative Ewing Thomason, who led the bill's defense, was merely to get some kind of bill voted out, since the administration was reasonably confident of being able to control the bill in conference committee. The four major Committee amendments passed with only military representation on the commission requiring a recorded vote. The other three disallowed the commission's authority to make grants-in-aid for research, struck the commission's information service (a favorite of scientists), and made security investigations more intensive and security penalties harsher. The House then adopted the bill, 265 to 79.

The Senate conferees (McMahon, Russell, Johnson, Vandenberg, and Millikin) agreed to the more stringent security penalties added by the House, and the House conferees (led by May) agreed to restore provisions for exchange of information on industrial applications of atomic energy. Relying on solid technical arguments, Senator Millikin successfully defended the Senate provision on patents (AEC ownership, with nonrestrictive licenses). The conferees then "traded" amendments on what had become the major issue in later debate on the commission, "civilian control" versus "military representation." Vandenberg prevailed in what at that point was his opposition to military representation on either the commission or its staff,[12] thus striking two of the three House Military Affairs Committee amendments, but the third major House amendment was left in, when the Senate conferees accepted the requirement that the director of the military applications division be an active military officer. On July 26, both houses accepted the conference report, and on August 1, 1946, President Truman signed the bill creating the civilian-controlled Atomic Energy Commission.

This is an example of policy initiation where everybody sees the need and desires that some sort of legislation be the outcome, but only after a policy "crisis" intervenes, namely, the news of the Hiroshima explosion. Before atomic energy went public, there was no such consensus, and the major impetus for consideration of postwar questions related to atomic energy was the desire of the Chicago atomic scientists to maintain their organization.[13] Major actors—the President, Bush, and Conant—took considerable time sorting out what policies they wanted to pursue. To contemporary students of

---

12. This is, of course, inconsistent with Vandenberg's earlier flirtations with pro-military amendments, but entirely consistent with what Dean Acheson has characterized as Vandenberg's ability and (presumably overriding) interest in putting his thumbprint on legislation:

> Arthur Vandenberg . . . was born to lead a reluctant opposition into support of governmental proposals that he came to believe were in the national interest. A leader should be in advance of his followers, but not so far in advance as to be out of touch. It helps, also, if he can believe in his own little stratagems. One of Vandenberg's stratagems was to enact publicly his conversion to a proposal, his change of attitude, a kind of political transubstantiation. The method was to go through a period of public doubt and skepticism; then find a comparatively minor flaw in the proposal, pounce upon it, and make much of it; in due course propose a change, always the Vandenberg amendment. Then, and only then, could it be given to his followers as true doctrine worthy of all men to be received. . . . Its strength lay in the genuineness of his belief in each step. He was not engaged in strategy; rather he was a prophet pointing out to more earthbound rulers the errors and spiritual failings of their ways.

Dean Acheson, *Present at the Creation* (New York: Norton, 1969), p. 223.

13. This has a private-sector analogue in the series of innovations that produced the new computer described by Tracy Kidder in *The Soul of a New Machine* (New York: Avon, 1981), pp. 36ff. In this case, the desire of engineers to remain in Westborough, Massachusetts, rather than move to a new unit in North Carolina was instrumental in determining the shape and scope of the project that eventuated in the new machine.

national politics, the comparative anemia of presidential leadership on this issue is instructive. Both the Royall-Marbury and the Newman drafts that formed the basis for rival congressional proposals were administration bills. President Truman even came fairly close to endorsing each at different times, although there is no question that after he had been alerted to the presidential stake in preserving control over the Atomic Energy Commission, he came down firmly for the Newman proposal. Nevertheless, presidential decision-making seems to have played only a minor role in the initiation of this policy. Much more important were (1) the desires of members of Congress to participate in establishing a policy once the news of the existence of atomic energy was out; (2) the contending military and scientific groups within the government; (3) the strategic placement of James Newman; and (4) the ambitious maneuvering of Senator Arthur Vandenberg, who also advocated inconsistent points of view at different times. In the end, of course, President Truman's influence was heavy, since it was impossible for the service Secretaries to oppose him directly. But without Newman's and Snyder's willingness to act in part as pipelines for scientific activists, the President might never have been alerted in time to his interests in the legislation, preoccupied as he was by his higher priority tasks of learning his job, ending the war, and negotiating complex peace settlements.

One would expect that when the stages of initiation and enactment are intermingled, as in this case, politicians would play a far greater role than experts in the innovation process. Politicians, however, are frequently distracted and cannot do their homework as thoroughly as experts. Their perception of the stakes may consist only of a desire to preserve an entitlement to participate rather than anything more substantive. So in this case, it appears that while politicians defined the need for a policy, it was staff members who actually supplied the policies over which political leaders clashed.

2. THE CREATION OF THE NATIONAL SCIENCE FOUNDATION

Many of the same forces that were at work in the creation of a civilian-controlled atomic energy commission also played a significant part in the establishment of the National Science Foundation. It was not until May of 1950, however, that President Truman signed the NSF bill into law, thereby putting on a new footing the responsibility of the federal government to fund and to encourage basic research in the natural sciences. That science was useful for solving national problems was not a World War II discovery.[14] Throughout American history, and particularly in times of war or crisis, scientists had been called upon for aid and had received federal support in return. Two such transactions, for example, in the North and the South respectively, had resulted in the development of the ironclad warships the *Merrimack* and the *Monitor*, which starred in a comic-opera naval engagement during the Civil War. But the idea that the government had a continuing responsibility for the support and development of "pure" science, basic research unrelated to any immediate problem or specific policy, was fairly new, at least in the form in which it found wide currency in both the scientific and governmental communities only shortly prior to the establishment of the National Science Foundation.

Several needs had to surface before the idea of federally supported basic research could become practical. First and most obvious was the need of scientists for money. This need, while not new, became critical during the 1930s as the costs of basic physical research increased. Modern science began to require increasingly expensive tools, and more people to operate them. Meanwhile, the funds available from private institutions and philanthropies decreased under the impact of the depression. Everyone has needs during a depression, and it was only when the needs of scientists were shown to complement and support the tasks of the government that government support of science began to be a significant governmental goal. Thus the government's need for a federal agency to coordinate previously disparate scientific efforts in combating the problems of the depression was quickly recognized and quickly met in 1933. But when the scientific community noted their need of money for basic research, a corresponding interest did not appear.

Efforts to obtain federal support during the 1930s, while themselves unsuccessful, had some educational value. Many scientists involved in this effort underwent a "school of hard knocks" education

14. Dupree, *Science*, pp. 1–19.

in American politics that provided them with experience and expertise helpful to their ultimate success.[15] By the late 1930s the needs of science were being cast in the language of the public interest, and an increasing number of federal officials had been persuaded. Although still not formally funded, federal support for basic research was, by 1940, widely accepted as reasonable. At the onset of the war, the needs of science suddenly received high priority. Precedents, institutional habits, and communications patterns were developed in an unplanned, haphazard way by the wartime Office of Scientific Research and Development (OSRD), which later provided the hothouse in which the postwar NSF grew.

In the postwar period 1945–50, the actual discussion of the NSF took place. By then, a sense of urgency about the care and feeding of scientists had died down. In its place there began to take hold a new concern on the part of scientists over government control of research and the problem of secrecy, and a corresponding mistrust of scientists in many parts of the government. While there was almost total consensus on the desirability of something like an NSF in 1945, a period of prolonged bargaining on the mechanisms of implementation dominated the next five years.

In the 1930s, federal aid had been given to research in an uncoordinated fashion by many departments and branches of the government, most visibly through the Department of Agriculture's attempts to spur agricultural productivity. But unlike the war, which stimulated science as well as disrupting it, the depression cast a cloud over the belief in the general usefulness of science. Many held scientific research to blame for depression-year agricultural overproduction when it occurred.

Responsibility for the revival of a federal concern for basic research apparently lies with two Roosevelt cabinet members, Harold Ickes of Interior and Henry Wallace of Agriculture.[16] Both men, and Ickes especially, saw themselves as concerned with problems of conserva-

15. See, for example, various accounts of the experiences of E. O. Lawrence, inventor of the cyclotron. Herbert Childs, *An American Genius* (New York: Dutton, 1968); and Nuel Pharr Davis, *Lawrence and Oppenheimer* (New York: Simon and Schuster, 1968), especially pp. 39–41, 47, 69–74, 86, 90, 94–95.

16. This account follows closely that provided in Dupree, *Science*, pp. 344–381.

tion, and both turned to research for solutions to these problems. The result was increased interest in, and later support for, federal aid to basic research, and an increasing recognition that coordination of research would be necessary if the problems were ever to be attacked successfully.[17]

The need for coordination and funding was brought to Secretary Wallace's attention by the geographer Isaiah Bowman, President of The Johns Hopkins University and head of the National Research Council (NRC), a committee established by Congress during the first World War to provide a link between those possessing scientific knowledge and persons formulating military needs. The NRC was accustomed to work primarily along lines established by the fields of science themselves, rather than around the scientific and administrative problems of government. Organized by disciplines, not "problem areas," NRC advice to the government on problems such as soil conservation and flood control lacked the broad scope of the scientific community's potential contribution that an interdisciplinary board might have provided. When Bowman was approached by Wallace with regard to an effort being made in the Agriculture Department to reorganize the Weather Bureau, Bowman responded that the NRC might not have the appropriate information readily available. He suggested instead that a general board be established to appoint committees to deal with specific problems as they occurred within the departments of government. The close connections of the NRC with the National Academy of Science had meant that the effectiveness of the former was largely dependent upon feelings within the latter. The new board, Bowman felt, might be a way of securing the necessary responses more quickly.

Wallace agreed and transmitted the proposal to President Roosevelt. The President created a Science Advisory Board (SAB) with authority to appoint committees to deal with specific problems in the various departments. In July 1933, Roosevelt appointed Karl Compton, President of the Massachusetts Institute of Technology, to head the newly formed body. The Board was not federally financed, but instead received its support through the machinery of the National

17. See, for an example of research in the service of conservation, the erosion experiment stations of the Bureau of Soils. Arthur Schlesinger, Jr., *The Coming of the New Deal* (Boston: Houghton Mifflin, 1959), pp. 335–353.

Academy and the NRC with additional aid from the Social Sciences Division of the Rockefeller Foundation. As it functioned under Compton and Bowman, the Board saw its role as fulfilling the functions that the National Academy had originally set for itself but failed to achieve, that is, to act as an independent group of scientists not in the government, but able to comment on the work of the federal research establishment.[18] In this role the Board studied the coordination of the government's scientific bureaus, made inquiries to uncover unnecessary duplications of effort, and made general recommendations for the more efficient use of scientific personnel.

But Compton had other ideas as well. Soon after the Board was established, it issued a report, "Recovery Program of Science Progress," calling for some $16 million to be spent over a six-year period in support of research. Most of this money was justified as applied research necessary for Public Works projects (e.g., to make programs such as the CCC more effective), but a significant portion was reserved for basic research grants in an effort to alleviate unemployment among scientists themselves. When no response from the President was forthcoming, Compton again argued for federal support programs in late 1934, now setting the required funding levels at some $15 million per year. That same year, Compton became President of the American Association for the Advancement of Science (AAAS), the largest membership group of scientists in the United States, and mobilized its support behind his proposal.

President Roosevelt passed the buck and Compton's proposal to Secretary of the Interior Ickes. Ickes sent the proposal to the National Resources Board, a group established initially to confer on the role of science in national planning. The Board, which Ickes chaired, was divided between men whose concern was basically applied science (including FDR's uncle, Frederick Delano, an eminent city and regional planner) and men who felt that any sensible planning involved long-range basic research. Unfortunately for Compton's proposal, most of those who agreed with his concern for basic research were also social scientists (among the most prominent, University of Chicago political scientist Charles Merriam). Suspicious of the exclusion of social science proposals in the Compton report, they saw the

18. Dupree, *Science*, pp. 350–351.

Science Advisory Board more as a special interest group of natural scientists than as a body concerned with the support of all science. The National Resources Board finally recommended to the President that support be given only to specific (applied, not basic) research projects, and that this be limited to work carried on by the government, not by private institutions. These recommendations were adopted by FDR in January of 1935. The SAB was disbanded some six months later.

Those members of the National Resources Board interested in support for basic research did not give up, however, on efforts for a more inclusive proposal for federal aid to science. Reconstituted in June 1935 as a larger and more social science—oriented committee (now called the National Resources Committee), its members undertook a large-scale study of the relation of government to intellectual life in the United States—including, among other matters, the place of science. The result, published in 1937, was the report *Research— A National Resource,*[19] an effort that pointed out the dependency of government research projects on the total research resources of the nation. The implication that government had a greater responsibility to "private" institutions and individuals than had previously been thought was drawn for the benefit of government officials. The report argued that the needs of the government were now so large that private institutions could not handle them without aid of a fundamental sort, and hence that support for applied research was inseparable from support for basic research.

The approach of the war hastened the translation of these visible needs into government priorities. The National Research Council was a weak instrument for these purposes. It had no official position or broad support within the scientific community—the kind of support necessary to organize an emergency war effort—since it had broken with the Compton recommendations in 1935. Neither did it have the kinds of administrative powers or the status of a central scientific organization within the government that would have permitted it to act in an official capacity. Those scientists who worried about American capabilities in warfare had little contact with it, and

19. Science Committee to the National Resources Committee, *Research—A National Resource* (Washington, D.C.: Government Printing Office, 1938—41).

thus were unable to communicate their feelings to a government not yet visibly involved in preparation for war.

Members of the natural science community understood quite early the importance of technology in the upcoming battle. Further, and significantly, they believed not only that America would become involved, but that it should: many were refugees and many were Jewish and had a special consciousness of events in Nazi Germany. From 1939 on, most visibly in Einstein's famous letter to FDR,[20] but in similar incidents that were repeated in almost every part of the scientific community, scientists formed themselves into informal preparedness groups and attempted to awaken the government to the international threat and the consequent research needs of the next few years.

The most important among these groups, later the core of the National Defense Research Council (NDRC), was formed as a result of a pro-Nazi speech given by Charles Lindbergh in 1940.[21] Lindbergh, still an American hero, spoke eloquently about the need for American separation from the problems of Europe in public radio speeches. In a private meeting of engineers at the Carnegie Institution in Washington, he graphically described the technical invincibility of the German war machine.[22] In his Carnegie audience were men

20. The letter is dated August 2, 1939. An extract is reprinted in Fermi, *Atoms in the Family*, opposite p. 198.

21. This account is taken from Robert Sherwood, *Roosevelt and Hopkins* (New York: Grosset and Dunlap, 1948), pp. 152–158.

22. As Sherwood puts it:

Because he had an exceptional understanding of the power of machines— as opposed to the principles which animate free men—he came to the seemingly logical conclusion that Nazi Germany was invincible and that Britain, France, the United States and everybody else should wake up and, facing the facts of modern life, yield to "the wave of the future." A retiring and taciturn man by nature as well as by force of cruel circumstance, Lindbergh became a violent and extremely eloquent crusader for the cause of isolationism. He was undoubtedly Roosevelt's most formidable competitor on the radio. . . . Lindbergh did not say much publicly at this time of what he had seen of German might and of British, French and Russian weakness. But when he recited facts and figures at private meetings he could generally scare the living daylights out of his listeners and some of them were impelled to write to Roosevelt urging him to command Churchill to surrender at once to prevent the impending carnage.
Ibid., p. 153.

who had long been aware that Germany had the capability for modern warfare. Now, thoroughly frightened by the realization that capabilities had been turned into achievements, they decided to act. Vannevar Bush, head of the Carnegie Institution, had been in contact with various like-minded scientists for some time and, spurred by Lindbergh's speech, proposed to these men that a plan for funding and coordinating American research be established. Bush, because of his location in Washington, was made chairman of this ad hoc group of scientists that included James Conant, then President of Harvard University, MIT President Karl Compton, former head of the defunct Science Advisory Board, and Frank Jewett, head of the National Academy of Sciences and chairman of the research division of Bell Telephone. These men had had some experience in both scientific and bureaucratic politics, and among them had contacts with many of the great foundations, universities, and scientific industrial firms. Together they drew up a plan for the National Defense Research Council, a body designed to fund and coordinate American efforts at achieving a war technology.

Bush arranged to present the proposal to Harry Hopkins, special assistant to the President and a major access route to FDR at this time. Hopkins, impressed as much by Bush as by the proposal, arranged a meeting with FDR in May of 1940. Roosevelt felt that a general rearmament effort would be aided by the recommendations of scientists. He formed the National Defense Research Council on June 15, 1940—the day after the fall of Paris—using the original ad hoc committee members as its staff.[23]

The NDRC took actions and made recommendations that set precedents for postwar government-science relations. Rather than build laboratories under the auspices of the government, they chose to act where possible along the lines first established by the National Cancer Institute in 1937, using the facilities of universities and industrial firms through contracts and promoting basic research by means of federal fellowships and grants. Although the NDRC re-

---

23. The NDRC itself had an important predecessor in the National Advisory Committee for Aeronautics, whose chairman was also Vannevar Bush. Dupree, *Science*, p. 370.

ceived many specific assignments from the military services, they were allowed to use independent judgment as to what could and should be funded, and how the task should proceed. For the first time, the government pursued the notion of funding basic research, not simply applications. At this time, they established the principle of no profit on discoveries. The NDRC (hence the government) would meet expenses of scientists through royalty-free use of discoveries by the government, but would not retain patents. These precedents all had their effect on the later design of the NSF.

But while an important step, the NDRC failed in many respects. For one thing, it was initially limited in its jurisdiction to weapons research. Other equally valuable approaches to war technology (e.g., in the fields of communications or medicine) were excluded. The organization was structured as a committee with the usual problems of inefficiency involved in obtaining quorums and making and executing decisions. Finally, a number of the recommendations of the Council were simply too abstract. The possibilities of several lines of weapon development were noted, but no plans for development appeared to follow. The need to supplement basic research on weapons with an equal effort in engineering development led, in June 1941, to the formation of the Office of Scientific Research and Development. The OSRD, headed by Bush, expanded the research scope of the old NDRC and tied it to problems of development as well. It was organized hierarchically, within the executive department, with Bush having full authority as director and answerable to the President.

As a wartime measure, the OSRD was extremely successful. It was administratively responsible for, among other things, the development of radar, the proximity fuse, and the atomic bomb. But it also produced a number of problems, frictions, and divisions that were to plague postwar efforts for a National Science Foundation. The hierarchical structure made wartime coordination possible, but it also decreased access for many elements of the scientific community. The decisions which Bush had to make and made alienated some scientists. Many pure scientists, for example, suffered under the increased emphasis on development at the expense of basic research. This was felt not only in the shortage of funds, but also in decreased protection from the draft as compared with presumably more essential scientific specialists.[24]

Problems like these produced a certain amount of resistance to the idea of a single presidentially appointed czar for science after the war, or to a hierarchical structure in general. Bush himself was sympathetic to those who felt critical of the organization he headed. As a citizen, he was concerned that the increasing emphasis on development—which he supported as a wartime necessity—would transform the OSRD into a simple adjunct of the military services. Because he realized that support for science in the wartime pattern would be neither possible nor desirable after the war, Bush opposed a postwar continuation of the OSRD.

In its place Bush envisioned a new governmental agency established along the lines of the old NDRC for the purpose of funding basic research. Hierarchy, distasteful but necessary in war, could be eliminated in peacetime. Relations with the military would be kept to a minimum. Secrecy, which most scientists had deplored during the war, would no longer be appropriate. Bush communicated his thinking along these lines to the President as early as the summer of 1944. There is also some indication that he realized that movement in this direction would be encouraging to those scientists who already were chafing under secrecy regulations and had become concerned over postwar control of atomic energy.

President Roosevelt wrote a letter to Bush on November 17, 1944, which set in motion the investigation leading to Bush's report, *Science: The Endless Frontier*,[25] with its suggestion of a National Research Foundation. The idea for the letter has been traced to Oscar Cox, general counsel of the Foreign Economic Administration, who was evidently interested in utilizing "war-time discoveries, research and development to create fuller peace-time employment" and not particularly in the postwar support of science. Cox had worked on the establishment of OSRD, and through Harry Hopkins suggested a letter from Roosevelt requesting Bush's views on support for postwar

24. Bush wrote after the war that he had encountered difficulties protecting even the key men in weapons laboratories. See Vannevar Bush, *Pieces of the Action* (New York: William Morrow, 1970), pp. 288–290.

25. Vannevar Bush, *Science: The Endless Frontier* (Washington, D.C.: Government Printing Office, 1945).

science. This in turn led to meetings between Bush, Cox, and the OSRD's general counsel, Oscar Ruebhausen, who shaped the final draft, in which Roosevelt asked Bush a series of questions reflecting concerns much broader than those of economic recovery: (1) How could scientific knowledge developed during the war be released quickly? (2) How could medical research be facilitated? (3) How could the government assist research by other organizations? and (4) Could a program of scientific education or training be developed?[26]

Though Bush did not originate the idea of the Roosevelt letter, he welcomed it in part because there was beginning to be congressional interest in postwar plans for science. Detlev Bronk, Isaiah Bowman's successor as President of Johns Hopkins and an early NSF-connected luminary, describes the congressional concerns that arose out of "an investigation of war production for the Senate Small Business Committee" by Herbert Schimmel, a University of Pennsylvania physicist. This was a study of rubber tires and possible shortages.

> Schimmel decided [Bronk says] that the government should equip itself with means to provide for its technological needs and should not rely completely on industries that had not been designed to care for a major war emergency. Consequently, he began to formulate plans for an office of technological mobilization that would secure world leadership in the practical application of scientific discoveries, stimulate new discoveries and inventions, mobilize all technical facilities, and compel the licensing of all patents at reasonable compensation in order to foster their wide utilization. He suggested those plans to Senator Kilgore whom he had met while the senator was investigating the rubber program as a member of the National Defense Investigating Committee, better known as the Truman Committee. Kilgore was favorable to Schimmel's suggestion and with the approval of Senators Truman and Pepper sponsored the first Technological Mobilization Bill, S. 2721, in August 1942.[27]

Thereafter Kilgore maintained a steady interest in the problem, repeatedly introducing bills and holding hearings on wartime and postwar scientific mobilization.

26. J. Merton England, "Dr. Bush Writes a Report: Science—the Endless Frontier," *Science* 191 (January 9, 1976): 41–47.

27. Detlev W. Bronk, "The National Science Foundation: Origins, Hopes, and Aspirations," *Science* 188 (May 2, 1975): 409–410.

Bush immediately responded to the Roosevelt letter by forming four task forces of scientists, government officials, and educators to tackle each question and report back to him. Panel chairmen were Irvin Stewart, a lawyer who was executive director of the OSRD, Dr. Walter Palmer of Columbia Medical School, President Isaiah Bowman of The Johns Hopkins University, and Henry Allen Moe of the Guggenheim Foundation. Bronk says:

> They were aided by two score eminent scientists who worked steadily on the four committees throughout the early months of 1945. From their reports evolved *Science: The Endless Frontier*.[28]

As envisioned by Bush, the purpose of a National Science Foundation would be to

> develop and promote a national policy for scientific research and scientific education . . . support basic research in nonprofit organizations . . . develop scientific talent in American youth by means of scholarships and fellowships, and . . . by contract and otherwise support long-range research on military matters.[29]

Included in the recommendations of the Bush report were three of the points later to become matters of major controversy. First, the scope of the proposed organization was to be limited to the hard sciences: social science was excluded.[30] Second, and most controversial, Bush recommended that the organization be headed by a director appointed by a part-time board of scientists. The scientists would be appointed by the President, but would not otherwise be connected with the government. These scientists would, in addition, have the power to appoint heads of the five divisions of the Foundation (medicine, defense, basic research, scholarships, publications), from recommendations submitted by the National Academy of Science. Finally, Bush recommended that the new organization continue the wartime policy of the OSRD on the patentable results of government-sponsored research: the inventor (or his employers)

28. Ibid., p. 410.
29. Bush, *Science: The Endless Frontier*, p. 115.
30. For a more extensive discussion on the NSF and social science, see Gene M. Lyons, *The Uneasy Partnership* (New York: Russell Sage Foundation, 1969), pp. 126–136, 269–277.

would retain the private patent rights, but the government would be given a royalty-free license for governmental purposes under any patents resulting from work financed by the Foundation.

Both the Roosevelt and the Truman administrations had been and continued to be favorable to the idea of federal funding for basic research. Their view of the scope of the agency, its administrative organization, and the problems of patent rights, however, diverged from Bush's recommendations. The Director of the Bureau of the Budget, Harold Smith, and his aide on scientific matters, Don K. Price, made their wishes known in conferences with Bush and with Senator Kilgore. For several reasons Bush decided not to compromise in advance negotiations; this decision was to contribute to the five-year delay in the establishment of the National Science Foundation.

First, the differences between Bush and the administration over the organization of the Foundation were quite basic. President Truman wished the internal structure of the Foundation to be set up along the hierarchical pattern of the OSRD, with a director appointed by (and responsible to) the President. He felt that the committee structure of the Bush proposal was not only unwieldy, but also lacked the lines of responsibility that any governmental agency should have. Second, as a result of the urging of Price, a political scientist, and others, Truman favored the inclusion of the social sciences within the scope of the Foundation. Finally, Truman favored government retention of any discoveries made through Foundation support.[31]

As important as these differences were, Bush might have been willing to compromise on them for the sake of a workable bill but for two considerations. First, it appeared that support for basic research would be forthcoming whether or not a National Science Foundation was immediately established. Early in 1944, the Army and the Navy had set up joint committee hearings chaired by Charles Wilson of the General Electric Company to enquire into the needs of postwar military scientific research. That committee had recommended the formation of an independent research board, funded through military appropriations, to contract for research in areas having potential

31. The differences between Truman and Bush are dealt with at length by Don K. Price, *Government and Science* (New York: New York University Press, 1954), pp. 32–64.

military use.[32] To this end, a bill was introduced by Harry Byrd, chairman of the Naval Affairs Committee in July of 1945. With the appearance of the Bush report and the idea of a much broadened national commitment to science over and above merely military applications, the military had temporarily dropped its push for special legislation. In 1946 the Office of Naval Research (ONR) was established as a statutory bureau funded through military appropriations. Through the ONR, the Navy, directly after the war, did a sizable portion of the job that Congress was considering allocating to the NSF, funding basic research (not simply military applications) through a system of grants and contracts. Thus both the scientific establishment and the military, the two major clients of the NSF, had created a working arrangement that allowed them the luxury of waiting for "satisfactory" legislation from Congress. The pressure for compromise was, as a consequence, greatly diminished for Bush and his supporters.[33]

The second important reason for Bush's refusal to give in on the administration's demands was that he felt he could win without compromise. To a majority of scientists, the idea of a presidentially appointed director smacked of political control of science—a problem to which they had become sensitized during debates over wartime secrecy and, later, over the problem of control of atomic energy. Many scientists did not profess to understand the questions involved, but chose to trust Bush, an engineer and professional science administrator, to represent the interests of science better than Truman. Bush also had the support of the "scientific establishment." His report made it obvious (through the qualifications set for members of the Board) that the new Foundation would be controlled mainly by the same major scientists from the larger institutions who had played such an important part in the management of wartime research. Bush also proposed that foundation grants be made on merit to institutions, rather than on some geographic or spoils basis, and this made it appear likely that the scientifically better off would maintain their

32. J. A. Furer, "Post-War Military Research," *Science* 100 (November 24, 1944): 461–464.

33. Price, *Government*, pp. 58–59. Cf. also the first chapter of Bruce L. R. Smith, *The Rand Corporation* (Cambridge: Harvard University Press, 1966) for a parallel Air Force story.

positions. Finally, Bush's recommendation of private retention of
patent rights gave him the support of prospective private industry
contractors, their peak organization, the National Association of
Manufacturers (NAM), and to a lesser but still important extent, the
Secretaries of the Army and the Navy, who had found this approach
helpful in gaining the support of industry and educational institutions
for research activities during the war.[34]

These reasons, together with President Truman's apparent political weakness in the Seventy-ninth Congress, prompted Bush to
ignore Kilgore and the administration's wishes. Rather, he enlisted
the support of Senator Warren Magnuson (whose important constit-
uent, Boeing Aircraft, favored both the board proposal and the patent
provisions). In July 1945, Magnuson submitted a bill containing the
basic proposals of the Bush report. Four days after the introduction of
the Magnuson-Bush package, Senator Kilgore introduced his own
bill, containing the recommendations of the administration.

In addition to those differences already mentioned, Kilgore's proposal further alienated the Bush group by requiring that funds be
distributed geographically as well as by merit. It was supported by
the Association of Land Grant Colleges and by senators from the
more sparsely populated states. In line with the wishes of the President, Kilgore also broadened the scope of the proposed Foundation
to include the social sciences. Thus, by the beginning of October
1945, there were two distinct alternative proposals for an NSF before
Congress (table 2.1).

On November 30 of that year, the Committee in Support of the
Bush Report was formed, headed by the chairman of one of Bush's
original advisory committees, Isaiah Bowman. This group was characterized by the administration as involving a "small, inner group of
scientists, closely allied with a few powerful institutions and large
corporations"[35] where most of the war research had been conducted.
Its purpose was to gain the support of the scientific community for the
Magnuson proposal. About one month later, a larger group of scien-

---

34. Cf. Howard Meyerhoff, "The Truman Veto," *Science* 106 (September 12, 1947);
"Memorandum of J. Donald Kingsley to John R. Steelman of December 31, 1946," in
James L. Penick, ed., *The Politics of American Science* (Chicago: Rand McNally,
1965), pp. 72−73; Smith, *Peril*, pp. 437−444.

35. Kingsley memorandum in Penick, ed., *Politics*, p. 73.

Table 2.1. Two Proposals for a National Science Foundation, 1945

	Bush-Magnuson	Kilgore-Truman
Scope	Physical sciences and health	Physical sciences, health, and social sciences
Organization	Director appointed by Board; Board appointed by President, but with no other government connections or responsibilities	Director appointed by and responsible to President
Fund Dispersal	By merit	By geography and population
Patent Rights	Owned by discoverer, with royalty-free government use	Owned by government, with possibility of nonexclusive free licenses
Supporters	Big science, military, National Assocation of Manufacturers, industry	Administration, land grant colleges

tists, headed by Harold Urey of Columbia, formed the Committee for a National Science Foundation in support of the Kilgore proposal. This group desired to avoid the further concentration of research and the power to control research that such concentration implied.

Joint hearings on both bills were held by Magnuson and Kilgore in the fall of 1945 through January 1946. During this period the Bush group won a few points and conceded a few until, by the end of February, a compromise proposal appeared to have been agreed upon. Accordingly, in February Senator Kilgore introduced a new bill, which retained the single administrator but gave the advisory board more power, as in the Magnuson bill, by making it smaller and able to make recommendations to the President and Congress. The Magnuson patent provisions were largely accepted, although with somewhat greater retention of governmental control. The geographical distribution requirement was cut back (only 25 percent of the funds now had to be so dispersed), and the proposal was shorn of its provision for social science research. This bill, S. 1850, had the approval of the Bush and Urey groups, and the support of Senator Magnuson. It passed the Senate early in July.

Bolstered by the opposition of some leaders in the field of medical sciences (who feared any type of government support would produce government control), and by the opposition of the NAM to the patent provisions of the compromise bill, Bush reneged on his promise of support for S. 1850. Bush evidently hoped that he could get his original proposal through the House, and thereby gain further concessions from the administration in the conference report. Accordingly, he induced Representative Wilbur Mills (D-Ark.) to introduce the original Magnuson bill (the Bush Report recommendations). It was referred to the Subcommittee on Public Health of the Interstate and Foreign Commerce Committee, which held a series of hasty hearings, initially leaving no chance for opponents to testify. The Subcommittee reported the bill favorably to the full Committee in July, but in an election year the bill got no further.

In October 1946, President Truman established, by executive order, a Scientific Research Board and appointed his personal assistant, John R. Steelman, as its head. The Board was officially charged with the investigation of existing federal research programs and was responsible for recommendations about their administration. Its report served to make Truman's position visible to the scientific community over the next two years of continuing controversy.

The larger scientific community had supported the efforts at compromise represented by S. 1850. The AAAS had expressed generalized support for the idea of an NSF, and its executive council had endorsed the Kilgore compromise by a vote of 230 to 10 after it had been favorably reported in the Senate. But the AAAS as a broad-spectrum professional society was neither prepared nor inclined to take the kinds of effective action that the recently formed Federation of Atomic Scientists (FAS) had taken with regard to the controversy over domestic control of atomic energy. The FAS, although it favored the passage of S. 1850, was also pressing at this time for action on the McMahon bill (AEC) and had to make a choice as to where its energies should be expended. Thus little happened on the NSF. The majority of scientists outside the government who were taking an interest in politics were convinced that the need to control atomic energy constituted an emergency so great that even the related problem of a national framework for research should be subordinated to it.

In the closing weeks of the Seventy-ninth Congress, the crisis that marked the fight for civilian control so absorbed the more articulate members of the American scientific community that the tabling of science legislation caused no great outcry.[36]

In December of that year, however, after the election, the FAS began to shift its attention from the McMahon bill to concern with the National Science Foundation, which they perceived as an alternative to purely military support of science. Initially their concern involved no more than participation in the Inter-Society Committee, an alliance of the various professional scientific societies. But at the same time, the FAS authorized its Washington branch, a group composed primarily of scientists working for the government, to examine and report on the purely political aspects of the various bills and their prospects for passage.

In February 1947, two science foundation bills were referred to the Senate Committee on Labor and Public Welfare, chaired by Majority Leader Robert A. Taft (R-Ohio). The first was the reintroduction of S. 1850 (the Kilgore compromise), which had passed the Senate the previous year. The second bill was introduced by Senator H. Alexander Smith (R-N.J.) at the request of Taft, who desired a bipartisan bill without the controversial features of S. 1850. Specifically, Smith's bill eliminated all provisions for geographical distribution of funds,[37] made patent rights subject to negotiation, and, most important, eliminated the presidentially appointed director in favor of an independent board. In the House, S. 1850 was introduced by Representative Emmanuel Celler (D-N.Y.), while the Smith bill was introduced by Representative Mills.

In hearings before the House Subcommittee on Public Health, administration representatives clearly favored the Celler bill (S. 1850) in all areas except patent policy, where they were willing to

36. Smith, *Peril*, p. 144: This book provides a convenient summary of legislative action on science proposals during this period.

37. See "News and Notes," *Science* 105 (April 18, 1947). Opponents of this dispersion by "merit" of funds desired some (if not all) of the available money be distributed on a geographic-population basis. That is, each state would get some minimum amount with the remainder being distributed on a population basis. For a rationale, see Clarence A. Mills, "Distribution of American Research Funds," *Science* 107 (February 6, 1948): 129.

accept the Smith patent provision of arrangements specific to each contract. This provision would gain in feasibility if the director of the Foundation were responsible to the President and not, as the Smith bill proposed, to an independent board of directors. Vannevar Bush predictably testified in favor of the Smith bill and endorsed its strong-board approach. In late March, the Smith bill was sent to the floor of the Senate, having been amended in committee over Taft's objection to give the President the right to appoint the director. On the floor, Senator Wayne Morse of Oregon successfully added a requirement that 25 percent of the funds be geographically dispersed. Efforts to include the social sciences and to revise the patent provisions were defeated.

In mid-July, the House passed an unamended Smith bill, excluding the geography requirement and the presidentially appointed director. In conference, the House prevailed on all points. The conference report then passed both houses. In September, Truman vetoed the bill, citing as his reason both the unwieldiness of the proposed board and its lack of accountability to the President.

Truman's veto message and the report of the Steelman Committee (issued in late August) alerted large numbers in the scientific community to the administration position for the first time. Up to this point, the membership of the FAS and the AAAS had been largely willing to accede to Bush's position simply because of his great prestige. For a number of reasons, this attitude began to erode.

In 1947, the Washington branch of the FAS attacked the Bush view through its *Bulletin of Atomic Scientists* as an attempt to make science an auxiliary of industry.[38] Truman's case was for the first time made by scientists, not by people unrelated to science. Also, scientific suspicions of government "control" had been undergoing a change similar to that which had taken place in the business community over the previous fifteen years. The relations of the scientific community with the Office of Naval Research, a major source of postwar funding (along with the Manhattan Project and the Atomic Energy Commission), had been extremely good. A high degree of academic freedom had been maintained in this program. It was so

38. "Toward a National Science Policy?," *Bulletin of the Atomic Scientists* 3 (December 1947): 357–358, 369.

successful, in fact, that the chief scientist of the ONR, Alan Water-
man, was later to become the natural choice for first director of the
NSF. It was also true that years of involvement with government had
changed the attitudes of some scientists: they no longer felt that the
government was something alien, in part because dealings with the
government now involved dealing with scientists who had been
recruited to government work.[39]

Taken in combination—the changes in attitudes, the report of the
Washington FAS group, a blast at Bush's intransigence by Howard
Meyerhoff, the executive director of the AAAS[40]—all these forces
began to work in favor of the administration's position. In late December 1947 and early January of the following year, a series of
conferences were held between members of the executive committee of the Inter-Society group, the relevant congressmen, Don Price
of the Bureau of the Budget, and Bush. Two different plans were
discussed. Bush urged legislation similar to the Smith bill, with
modifications designed to assure Truman's approval. Specifically, a
Foundation board of twenty-four members to be appointed by the
President, who would be requested to consider the recommendations of the National Academy, and a director appointed by and
responsible to the President.

The second proposal was offered by the FAS, and was basically the
unaltered Kilgore bill. The FAS argued that most scientists would
favor this approach (undoing all the compromises gained by Bush and
his associates over the past few years), but were persuaded that
politically there would be a better chance to obtain a Foundation
through modifications of a plan already approved by the Congress.

Thus, in late March of 1948, Senator Smith reintroduced his bill of
1947 with the modifications. The bill was reported out of committee
in less than a month, and passed the Senate several days later without
a dissenting vote. The House Interstate and Foreign Commerce
Committee also reported the bill favorably, but there progress
ended. The House Rules Committee, then smitten by one of its
periodic concerns over budgeting,[41] bolstered by NAM opposition

39. Smith, *Peril*, pp. 520ff.
40. Meyerhoff, "The Truman Veto," *Science* 106 (September 12, 1947): 236.
41. "News and Notes," *Science* 110 (September 9, 1949): 263.

and also the opposition of certain firms, principally Bell Telephone, that were concerned about the patent provisions, refused to report a rule for the bill. This stalemate, with Senate passage and House Rules Committee delay, continued through 1948 and all of 1949, until finally the bill bypassed the Rules Committee in 1950, under the twenty-one-day rule, and was enacted.

In this case, as in the last, we can see at work the powerful influence of policy entrepreneurs:[42] persons with special interests, competence, or expertise, who have a great deal to do with the alternatives considered and debated by more public figures. In the previous case James Newman played the predominant role, although Kenneth Royall and William Marbury were also extremely important. In the formation of the NSF, Vannevar Bush and Isaiah Bowman on one side, Don Price and Howard Meyerhoff on the other, all specialists capable of concentrating upon the details of policy, were significant in shaping—and timing—the final outcome.

The role of nonspecialist politicians can be distinguished from that of policy entrepreneurs. While specialists are focused upon the substance of policy and on the consequences of different arrangements for outcomes in the policy area, nonspecialist politicians concern themselves with more immediate political problems: who takes jurisdiction, who can take credit, and, more remotely, to whom an innovation grants power and other resources. At the latter point the focus of attention of specialists and nonspecialists may well converge, but the initial differences in their interests are also apparent.

3. THE NUCLEAR TEST BAN TREATY

The nuclear test ban was a treaty, and this of course entailed negotiations with foreign countries.[43] From the beginning, just after the existence of nuclear weapons became widely known, the entire American

---

42. See the useful discussion of policy entrepreneurs on congressional staffs by David Price in "Professionals and 'Entrepreneurs': Staff Orientations and Policy Making on Three Senate Committees," *Journal of Politics* 2 (May 1971): 316–336; and *Who Makes the Laws?* (Morristown, N.J.: General Learning Co., 1972).

43. A detailed and authoritative account of this subject is contained in Glenn T. Seaborg, *Kennedy, Khrushchev and the Test Ban* (Berkeley and Los Angeles: University of California Press, 1981).

foreign and science policy establishment defined the problem of a test ban in much the same way. After meeting with initial Soviet resistance and after a change in American administrations, unanimity in the definition of the need for a treaty was lost and a slow process of rebuilding support took place. Ultimately, agreement on the treaty's provisions between the USSR and the United States did not become possible until both possessed large stockpiles of thoroughly tested atomic weapons, and the concerns of policymakers in both nations shifted to the problem of controlling the spread of nuclear weapons to other countries.

Within the United States, the acceptability of alternatives varied as different interest groups and officials weighed the effects of radioactive fallout against the risks of secret Soviet tests, the possibility of effective policing mechanisms against general worries about the long-run cooperativeness of the Russian government.

As unanimity in official circles collapsed, the issue emerged from the inner councils of committee politics. Interest groups solicited ideas, took sides, attempted to arouse public opinion, engaged in research to support their views, and spread elaborate justifications on the record. This provides a vivid contrast to the hasty inside bargaining that took place over civilian control of atomic energy.

The issue of a nuclear test ban was only a part of the general problem of postwar disarmament about which the United States and the Soviet Union had much difficulty in reaching agreement. As we have seen, the scientific community expressed early concern over a potential arms race, and many scientists felt nuclear weapons posed a distinct and immediate threat to the survival of mankind, even before the actual bombing of Hiroshima.

Vannevar Bush was among the first of those in the Truman administration to press for an international agreement aimed ultimately at banning the production of nuclear weapons. The first step in Bush's plan was the creation of an international control agency. His opportunity to advocate this idea as United States policy came when Canada and Britain in 1945 requested a conference with the United States on international control of atomic energy, and Secretary of State Byrnes, caught without a policy, asked Bush to draft one, and to serve as an adviser at the conference.

United States policy in the immediate postwar period was further shaped by the Acheson-Lilienthal Report, the result of a committee headed by Undersecretary of State Dean Acheson and assisted by a technical panel headed by David Lilienthal, which had been asked by President Truman to develop a nuclear weapons policy. The Report, made public in 1946, reflected not only the ability of technical adviser J. Robert Oppenheimer to explain complex material to the panel, but also his clearly thought-out views on political problems, in its call for an international authority that alone would own or lease, mine and refine, and conduct research using all the world's supply of thorium and uranium and would have powers of inspection to guarantee this monopoly.

> In plain words, the Report sets up a plan under which no nation would make atomic bombs or the materials for them. All dangerous activities would be carried on—not merely inspected—by a live, functioning international Authority with a real purpose in the world and capable of attracting competent personnel. This monopoly of the dangerous activities by an international Authority would still leave a large and tremendously productive field of safe activities open to individual nations, their industries and universities. . . . [T]he extremely favored position with regard to atomic devices, which the United States enjoys at present, is only temporary. It will not last. We must use that advantage now to promote international security and to carry out our policy of building a lasting peace through international agreement.[44]

This proposal, with modifications from the staff of United States negotiator in the United Nations Bernard Baruch, served as the basis for United States policy in international meetings on the subject through the early 1950s. The Soviet response was to label it as an attempt by the United States to assure its continued domination in the atomic energy field, and the Soviet position was that the United States should cease weapon production and release all related technical information if it was sincere in its desire for international control. Discussions in which these points were made repeatedly went on

44. Department of State Press Release no. 274, April 23, 1946, quoted in Acheson, *Creation*, pp. 153–154.

from 1947 to 1954 under the auspices of the United Nations Commission for Conventional Disarmament.

Several dramatic incidents in 1954, plus major changes in the international military-political environment, served to lessen the relevance of earlier positions on control and to focus post-1954 discussion on more limited goals. In March 1954, fallout from a United States hydrogen bomb test endangered inhabitants of American Trust Territories in the Pacific and contaminated a Japanese fishing vessel. Shortly thereafter, fallout from a particularly large Soviet hydrogen bomb test came down in a radioactive rain on Japan. The worldwide reaction continued for nearly a year. The level of radioactive material in the air was the main focus of concern, but the facts that the most endangered nation appeared to be Japan, with its memories of nuclear holocaust, and that it was known that high radioactivity caused genetic damage, while it was not known what level caused how much damage, certainly added to the intensity of the reaction. The British Labour Party asked the United Nations to ban the testing of hydrogen bombs; Prime Minister Nehru of India asked the United States to halt bomb tests and requested the United Nations Disarmament Commission Subcommittee to arrive at an agreement to stop testing, even before a control system was worked out; the twenty-eight-nation Asian-African (Bandung) conference, able to agree on precious little in the way of specific recommendations, urged an agreement to end nuclear testing.

By 1954, the strategic environment had also changed. Both the United States and the USSR had amassed large stockpiles of nuclear weapons; it was thus no longer fruitful to try to ban their production, and there was no known inspection technique that would prevent their continued possession in secret even if a general disarmament proposal were agreed on. Atomic and conventional weapons had also become progressively less separable in strategic doctrines. The United States, particularly during the Eisenhower administration with its strategic reliance on "massive retaliation," was becoming highly dependent on atomic weapons in its continental defense and as a vital supplement to the NATO defense system and was not likely to agree to plans controlling the weapons themselves.

At the May 1955 Subcommittee meeting of the United Nations Disarmament Commission, the Soviet Union, while still proposing a total conventional and nuclear disarmament policy, acknowledged that no known detection system would guarantee discovery of a cache of atomic bombs and in effect backed off from its demand for immediate total disarmament by calling for a cessation of nuclear weapons tests as a first step to more comprehensive disarmament. Harold Stassen, United States Representative and Special Assistant for Disarmament to President Eisenhower, countered with an "open skies" proposal: the first step toward comprehensive disarmament should be development of a workable inspection system, to prevent surprise attacks and detect violations of future agreements. To meet these inspection needs, he proposed an exchange of blueprints of military establishments and aerial reconnaissance of each nation by the other. No agreement was reached on either proposal.

In March 1956, Soviet Premier Bulganin argued in a letter to President Eisenhower that a test ban required no control or inspection system since explosions could be detected anywhere in the world and publicly called for a test cessation, independent of disarmament progress in other areas. The United States denied that all tests were detectable and added a further condition for any ban: United Nations ambassador Henry Cabot Lodge said that any test ban would have to include not only a detection system, but also a cutoff in the manufacture of fissionable material.

The issue became important in the 1956 election campaign. Democratic presidential candidate Adlai Stevenson proposed a test cessation with an international control agency to be set up to detect violations, but without a curtailment of fissionable fuel or weapons production. The Federation of Atomic Scientists and Premier Bulganin publicly supported the proposal, but President Eisenhower argued that United States security would be jeopardized if an end to testing were not attached to a general disarmament agreement, and the proposal was fiercely ridiculed by Vice-President Nixon.

By 1957, however, opposition to atomic weapons testing was on the increase among the nonnuclear powers.

In March, the Japanese government decided to send Professor Masatoshi Matsushita, an eminent scientist, on a special mission to the U.S.S.R., the United Kingdom, and the United States, to urge a cessation of nuclear weapons tests. The following month, in a major address, Prime Minister Nehru renewed his appeal for a test ban, and he continued to urge such action throughout the year. Again in April the Labour Party in Britain . . . moved that the government should be requested to take immediate initiative and put forward effective proposals for the abolition of hydrogen weapon tests through effective international agreement. Later that month, eighteen of West Germany's leading nuclear physicists, including Professor Otto Hahn, the first to split the atom, signed a declaration that they would not participate in the construction or testing of weapons. On April 23, Dr. Albert Schweitzer issued an appeal through the Norwegian Nobel Committee which was broadcast in fifty countries . . . asking that public opinion demand an end to nuclear tests. Within a few days his appeal was endorsed by the Pope, and on May 10 the West German Bundestag adopted a resolution . . . urging the three nuclear powers to temporarily suspend their tests, pending the negotiation of an arms control agreement.[45]

Domestically, Adlai Stevenson continued to call for a test ban, a position in which he was joined by American socialist leader Norman Thomas. In February, the Federation of American Scientists proposed United States agreement to a ban without any linkage to general arms limitations; Linus Pauling, 1954 Nobel Prize—winner in chemistry, circulated a petition signed by two thousand scientists urging such an international agreement.

In June, Senator Mike Mansfield (D-Mont.) of the Senate Foreign Relations Committee proposed a summit conference to end tests of large nuclear weapons. In the same month, after holding hearings on the dangers of radioactive fallout, Representative Chet Holifield, chairman of the Special Subcommittee on Radiation of the Joint Committee on Atomic Energy, recommended that the United States unilaterally halt such tests, a position in which he was later joined by his Republican colleague Representative Sterling Cole.

The Subcommittee of the United Nations Disarmament Commission met in London from March to September 1957 to renew disarmament negotiations. The USSR announced that it would accept the United States condition of a control system to monitor a test cessation, and agreed to a two- or three-year ban rather than an unlimited

---

45. Harold K. Jacobson and Eric Stein, *Diplomats, Scientists, and Politicians* (Ann Arbor: University of Michigan Press, 1966), pp. 20–21.

one. United States negotiators agreed to place nuclear test cessation at the top of the agenda for discussion, even though United States reliance on nuclear arms was much greater than the Soviet Union's, owing to the very large Soviet conventional army. The United States also agreed to a suspension of testing while a control system was being established and hinted that the test ban issue could be divorced from general disarmament. Stassen urged this latter position on the President, but Eisenhower refused to separate the issues, on the advice of the chairman of the Atomic Energy Commission, Admiral Lewis Strauss, Secretary of Defense Charles Wilson, and Secretary of State John Foster Dulles.

The Soviets refused to link a test ban and general disarmament and disagreed with the United States desire for extensive controls to cut off production of militarily useful fissionable materials, a position in which it was joined by almost all Subcommittee members. In August, the United States did agree to British Foreign Secretary Selwyn Lloyd's proposal for a committee of technical experts to comment on technical aspects of the conference agenda, but the Soviet Union refused to participate in technical tasks until there was agreement on other facets of test cessation.

During these years of fruitless negotiation, American scientists were far from united on the nuclear weapons policy. Robert Gilpin has described three main schools of thought on the subject.[46] The basic division was between the "control" school, represented by such scientists as Linus Pauling and Harvard astronomer Harlow Shapley, who believed that continued development or possession of atomic weapons by either the United States or the Soviet Union made the world insecure, and the "containment" school, whose members felt that the cold war was caused by Soviet militarism and necessitated the United States' maintaining a clear military advantage. The containment school was itself subdivided into a finite containment group, which felt that containing Soviet aggression might still permit a carefully inspected international control agreement at some future time without jeopardizing world peace, and the infinite containment group, which entertained no such hope.

46. Robert Gilpin, *American Scientists and Nuclear Weapons Policy* (Princeton, N.J.: Princeton University Press, 1962).

> In contrast to the finite school which believed that a feasible control
> system could be developed even in a politically divided world, the
> infinite containment school . . . argued that control over nuclear weap-
> ons would only be possible in a completely open world such as that
> envisioned in the Baruch Plan. Under the conditions of modern sci-
> ence, the arms race would therefore be unavoidable until the political
> differences underlying that arms race were settled.[47]

By the mid-1950s, scientists of the finite containment school, for
whom Cornell physicist Hans Bethe was a frequent spokesman,
began to support a test ban, seeing it as preserving mutual deterrence
and simultaneously reversing a dangerous arms race. The infinite
containment group continued to maintain that until the Soviet Union
was an open society, partial control agreements would be only a
license for it to develop new weapons while the United States stood
still.

There was a tacit alliance between scientific advocates of control
and of finite containment by the beginning of the 1957 Disarmament
Commission Subcommittee talks, but the influence of this alliance
was diluted by the fact that the Eisenhower administration relied
heavily for scientific advice on the infinite containment school. AEC
Chairman Strauss, an ardent exponent of infinite containment, opposed any test ban agreement. He was joined in this position by the
rest of the AEC and by the chairman of the Joint Chiefs of Staff,
Admiral Arthur N. Radford, who opposed any agreements with the
Soviet Union. Gilpin comments that

> the President and Mr. Dulles were unwitting prisoners, in their lonely
> isolation at the top of the government pyramid, of the special selection
> of knowledge and attitudes which came to them through official chan-
> nels and especially through Mr. Strauss. They had no alternative
> against which to measure the partisan quality of this advice or its
> scientific inadequacies.[48]

This sort of allegation plays a large part in many accounts of
high-level decision-making. It implies that chosen policies may not
have been intended to be picked by decision-makers because characteristics of the decision-making process itself constrained awareness

47. Ibid., p. 102.
48. Ibid., p. 382. See also Bush, *Pieces of the Action*, pp. 307–308.

of alternatives. Since no decision-making is possible at all without some sort of closure, at least some constraint upon options is bound to be unavoidable under any circumstances. Historians thus must accept the responsibility of foreclosing the possibility that decision-makers are aware of at least some foregone alternatives and simply have chosen an alternative different from the one historians favor. In this instance, as in so many, President Eisenhower is perceived as innocently unwitting—and incompetent—rather than adjudged guilty of rationally pursuing his views, however mistaken, by, among other things, consciously choosing advisers who would give him advice he wanted to follow. The overall notion of Eisenhower as an unconscious manager of his administration has been sharply disputed and leads to the conjecture that he perfectly well knew what he was doing.[49]

Some outside experts were of course in full agreement with Strauss and Radford. When Senator Henry Jackson, chairman of the Military Applications Subcommittee of the Joint Committee on Atomic Energy, asked Ernest O. Lawrence, Mark Mills, and Edward Teller of the University of California Livermore Radiation Laboratory to speak to President Eisenhower on the development of a "clean" or neutron bomb, these scientists took the opportunity to press for continued nuclear testing. Eisenhower replied, however, that the fears of the world required the United States to follow through with its offer of test suspension under specified conditions.

Largely as a response to the Soviet Union's orbiting of Sputnik in early October 1957 (rather than as a response to the uniformity of scientific advice he received), President Eisenhower appointed James R. Killian, President of MIT and a member of the finite containment school, to a newly created post of Special Assistant to the President for Science and Technology. A few days later, he expanded the government's Scientific Advisory Committee and raised its status by putting it in the White House. The new committee was divided enough in its internal opinions to give the administration alternative views on United States armaments policy.

49. See Fred I. Greenstein, "Eisenhower as an Activist President: A Look at New Evidence," *Political Science Quarterly* 94 (Winter 1979–80): 575–599; and Robert A. Divine, *Eisenhower and the Cold War* (New York: Oxford University Press, 1981).

During 1958 and 1959 the "control—finite containment" alliance of scientists continued to advocate a test ban. A January 1958 petition organized by Linus Pauling was sent to the United Nations Secretary-General containing the signatures of nine thousand scientists from forty-three nations. In February there was a statement from the Federation of American Scientists urging that even small atomic weapons be incorporated into any agreements and asserting that a control system was feasible.

At an early 1958 National Security Council meeting, Secretary Dulles complained that the United States was suffering propaganda losses because of continued testing and would suffer more, should the United Nations General Assembly condemn nuclear testing. Killian suggested that the Scientific Advisory Committee study the issues, and Eisenhower asked him to set up a special panel to investigate the national security problems of a ban and the technical feasibility of a monitoring system. Hans Bethe was chosen to head the panel.

In March Dulles argued that the United States should unilaterally suspend testing since the Soviet Union was reliably reported to be considering doing so, and since he had advance word that the Bethe Panel would report that an agreement could be adequately inspected. Admiral Strauss and Deputy Secretary of Defense Donald Quarles opposed this and prevailed.

In early 1958 Congress began to take an interest in the problem. Senator Hubert Humphrey sponsored a resolution establishing a Subcommittee on Disarmament of the Senate Foreign Relations Committee. Under Humphrey's chairmanship, the Subcommittee held hearings through February, March, and April on the need for linking a test ban to arms control. Former Special Assistant Stassen told the Committee that they were separable issues. AEC member Dr. Spofford English stated that inspections for an agreement to end production of fissionable materials would have to be massive, but inspections for a test ban could be limited to less than twenty-five stations. He felt, however, that the danger was the production of nuclear weapons rather than their testing, and thus argued that the United States should attempt to control production first.

In late March, the Soviet Union completed its test series and announced a unilateral cessation, urging the United States to do likewise or face Soviet resumption. Eisenhower replied that the United States position on a test ban and disarmament was unchanged and suggested that a conference of technical experts be called to determine the capabilities of possible inspection systems; this time, the Soviets agreed to an East-West conference of experts. At about the same time, the Bethe Panel delivered its report, finding that while no inspection system would be foolproof, the risks to the United States of limited undetected cheating were acceptable.

The East-West Conference of Experts met on July 1 and agreed on the "Geneva System" for monitoring. This would consist of 170 land-based inspection posts, plus an international control commission that could make on-site inspections if an explosion were suspected.

An ad hoc group which came to be called the Committee of Principals—Secretary of State, Secretary of Defense, Director of the CIA, Chairman of the AEC, and Special Assistant to the President on Science—was responsible for formulating the United States' response to the experts' finding that inspection systems were feasible and desirable. The Principals took their by now standard positions on the two basic questions. On whether a test ban should be separated from the general disarmament issue, John Foster Dulles (State), Killian (Special Assistant), and Allen Dulles (CIA) favored separation, while Neil McElroy (Defense) and John McCone (AEC) did not; they divided the same way on whether the United States should suspend testing at once or await a signed agreement, three saying "at once," and two "later."

John Foster Dulles finally prevailed in setting administration policy: a test moratorium limited to one year, with future suspensions tied to more general disarmament. Eisenhower asked for three-way talks on these proposals, and the Soviets agreed, while charging that it would take the United States a year to be ready for any tests anyhow and claiming that the United States could not be sincerely interested in a ban since it continued to tie the ban to other arms control issues.

The Geneva Conference convened in late October 1958, and produced nothing besides agenda disputes and outright rejections. Senator Albert Gore, one of two congressional advisers to the United States delegation, returned to Washington and proposed publicly that the United States support essentially the "Kissinger formula" instead. In the October issue of *Foreign Affairs*,[50] Harvard political scientist Henry Kissinger had suggested that the United States try to agree with the Soviet Union to eliminate those tests that produced fallout and not attempt to reach agreement on "clean" surface, underground, and outer space tests, thus continuing United States military superiority. Gore altered this to a ban on all atmospheric tests, and suggested that it be inspected by each nation's own facilities; this would meet the problem of additional radioactive fallout, sidestep the problems of developing an international monitoring system, and allow the United States to continue weapons development, thus answering critics who claimed a test ban was a license for USSR military gains.

The United States began the reconvened Conference in January 1959 by arguing that the monitoring system suggested by the Conference of Experts was less reliable than claimed in detecting underground explosions, and that there were also problems in high-altitude tests. As a result, a second Conference of Experts was requested. The Soviet Union refused to convene a new technical conference, but agreed to continue negotiations and the test moratorium that went with them, when the United States announced its willingness to drop the condition that any ban be contingent on progress in other areas of disarmament.

In a mid-January press release, Senator Gore repeated his call for an atmospheric ban only. This position was supported in a letter to the President by the AEC, in Humphrey Subcommittee hearings by Senator Frank Church, and on the floor of the Senate by four additional senators. Pressure for a full ban was also present, however. Hans Bethe publicly asserted that an adequate inspection system was still feasible, Senator Humphrey expressed the same sentiments in a Senate floor speech, and Eleanor Roosevelt and twenty-one other prominent citizens did likewise in an open letter to international leaders.

In an attempt to keep the international discussions productive, British Prime Minister Harold Macmillan suggested to Premier

50. Henry A. Kissinger, "Nuclear Testing and the Problem of Peace," *Foreign Affairs* 37 (October 1958): 1–18.

Khrushchev that a certain number of on-site inspections could compensate for the newfound limitations to monitoring stations; both Khrushchev and Eisenhower stopped short of endorsing the idea, but showed interest.[51] In a further attempt to keep the United States seriously involved in finding a solution, Senator Humphrey sponsored a Senate resolution supporting United States efforts to negotiate a test ban, ostensibly as a means of countering Soviet propaganda.

> A more important effect of the resolution may well have been that in the context of the domestic debate, its adoption made it more difficult for the Administration to break off the negotiations. To do so might have seemed to defy the sense of the Senate. Establishing this inhibition may well have been Senator Humphrey's main motivation.[52]

As in the case of Arthur Vandenberg and civilian control of atomic energy, an enterprising senator, this time Humphrey, seized jurisdiction over an emerging issue by means of the establishment of a special subcommittee and then worked hard at keeping the possibility of a solution afloat in the world of policymakers.

In April President Eisenhower proposed two alternate routes to a test ban. Under the first plan, if the Soviets would change some procedural demands with respect to on-site inspections—principally the right of veto by the nation being inspected—and would discuss methods of detecting high-altitude tests, the United States would adopt a comprehensive test ban agreement. Under the second plan, a ban limited to atmospheric testing would be acceptable as a first step to a more comprehensive plan, if an international monitoring network were set up. This was unlike the Gore plan, which did not include international control of monitoring devices. Khrushchev rejected the second plan outright, but proposed that the first might be acceptable if Macmillan's quota system of on-site inspections could be negotiated; Soviet negotiators at Geneva implied that such a fixed number of inspections would make a veto unnecessary.

51. Eisenhower was urged to agree by Humphrey, who had returned from a visit with Khrushchev the previous December, at which time Khrushchev gave him certain atomic "secrets" for Eisenhower and left him optimistic about a test ban. Hubert H. Humphrey, "What Hope For Disarmament?," *New York Times Magazine*, January 5, 1958.

52. Jacobson and Stein, *Diplomats, Scientists, and Politicians*, p. 170.

Eisenhower's Committee of Principals was divided in their usual way on this proposal: the State Department, CIA, and Special Assistant on Science felt that on-site inspections would be sufficient assurance of Soviet compliance with the ban, while the Defense Department and the AEC did not. Eisenhower and Macmillan suggested additional technical working groups to discuss detection systems, the Soviets agreed, and technical discussion on the proposals continued as the regular sessions recessed. On the initiative of Khrushchev, however, the United States agreed to extend its test suspension during the talks, and the moratorium continued.

In late 1959, Senator Humphrey, still pressing the Republican administration from the outside, proposed that the United States make an agreement banning (1) all testing in the atmosphere, (2) high-altitude testing that could be monitored, (3) underwater testing of a certain yield, and (4) underground blasts of a certain yield. Additionally, there would be a two-year moratorium on underground tests of all types. In February 1960 the United States offered a new proposal at Geneva that followed Humphrey's ideas closely (down to the magnitude threshold); the major change was an inspection procedure similar to the Soviet quota system. The Soviets amended this to ban all tests except those underground; underground tests above the American magnitude figure were banned and subjected to inspection, providing there was a moratorium on underground tests below that yield, which would be enforced by the same on-site inspections.

This was almost exactly Humphrey's proposal and was also the plan the British were advocating. The first United States reactions were negative, from AEC chairman McCone and Senator Clinton P. Anderson (D-N.M.), chairman of the Joint Committee on Atomic Energy. But Hans Bethe came out publicly for it, Humphrey defended it on the floor of the Senate, and Macmillan flew to Washington to argue for it with Eisenhower. The AEC's usual ally in the Committee of Principals, the Defense Department, supported the proposal because it perceived a benefit in stationing inspectors inside Russia. The opposition of McCone alone was not enough to stem the tide this time. Eisenhower announced for the proposal, and the United States and Britain called for immediate efforts to effectuate it.

The remaining areas of disagreement were in the number of on-site inspections, the length of the moratorium, and obligations at the end of the moratorium, if detection systems for low-yield tests had not been developed. The Congressional Joint Committee on Atomic Energy began hearings on the technical problems of setting up a control system, primarily the question of whether on-site inspections could deter underground tests, about which there was some doubt.

On May 7, 1960, the Soviet Union announced the downing of a U-2 reconnaissance plane over its territory. Eisenhower, DeGaulle, and Macmillan were in the final stages of preparation for a Paris Summit Conference with Khrushchev aimed at a "general relaxation of tension," which might have included completion of a test ban agreement. President Eisenhower refused to condemn the flights, and test ban talks collapsed for the balance of the Eisenhower administration. Prime Minister Macmillan would later tell President Kennedy that the failure to achieve a test ban treaty "was all the fault of the American big-hole obsession and the consequent insistence on a wantonly large number of on-site inspections."[53]

The new Kennedy administration began negotiations at Geneva by proposing a version of the last Eisenhower proposal, altered to meet Soviet criticism—a ban on all high-altitude, outer-space, and underwater tests, a ban on all underground tests above a certain yield, and a moratorium on tests below that yield for three years while research into detection methods continued.

Soviet Ambassador Semyon Tsarapkin rejected the offer and injected a new issue—the structure of the international control organization. Previously, the Soviets had shown much less interest in this than had the Western participants. Now, however, the Soviets proposed a "troika" collective executive similar to the arrangement they were at that time attempting to impose on the United Nations. In his June meeting with Kennedy at Vienna, Khrushchev agreed to drop the demand for a "troika" control organization if a test ban and general disarmament could be solved together. This was a complete reversal of positions: in early negotiations, it was the United States that demanded that a test ban had to be coupled with disarmament agreements and the USSR that had been eager to discuss a test ban separately.

53. Arthur M. Schlesinger, Jr., *A Thousand Days: John F. Kennedy in the White House* (Boston: Houghton Mifflin, 1965), pp. 189–190.

United States negotiator Arthur Dean believed that the Soviet stance meant that they were about to resume testing. Kennedy was under some pressure to resume testing from the Joint Chiefs and some scientists, but he decided that the value of favorable world public opinion was higher and did not resume. On September 1, 1961, the Soviet Union announced resumption of testing. The United States and Britain countered by calling for an agreement to ban atmospheric tests producing fallout, the ban to be monitored by existing national systems; this was the first United States proposal that did not call for an international control system. It was rejected, and on September 5, Kennedy announced United States resumption of underground tests.

The final sessions of the Geneva conference met between November 1961 and January 1962 and are noteworthy only for the return of the major parties to their previous positions. Ambassador Tsarapkin called for a ban on atmospheric, high-altitude, outer-space, and underwater tests, to be monitored by national systems, and a moratorium on underground testing until control methods were devised. The United States reasserted a need for an international control system, contending that its September proposal was aimed only at preventing Soviet resumption of testing.

In 1962 the United States and the Soviet Union agreed to begin discussions of general disarmament under the auspices of the United Nations Disarmament Committee, thus shifting the arena to that eighteen-nation body. The Disarmament Committee created a subcommittee of the United States, United Kingdom, and USSR to develop a test ban treaty, but the usual deadlock over monitoring systems resurfaced. In an effort to end the deadlock and avert United States resumption of atmospheric testing, the eight neutral countries on the Committee, headed by Sweden and India, submitted a draft treaty, but it did not specifically resolve the areas of disagreement, and the United States resumed testing in April.

In late April, the United States began reformulating its position. Fallout from Soviet and American tests had reached a very high level. United States strategic policy was changing; the already large stockpiles reduced the value of future tests, and Kennedy was emphasizing development of conventional forces. The United States was becoming increasingly aware of the difficulties in detecting underground explosions and of the consequent probable low yield of on-site inspections. A committee consisting of the old Committee of Principals plus the Joint Chiefs of Staff came up with two draft proposals.

The first draft provided for a limited ban, proscribing atmospheric, outer-space, and underwater tests, with detection through national systems; this would control fallout and allow continued United States testing. The second draft was a comprehensive test ban treaty, with international coordination of national detection systems and some mandatory on-site inspections. In August the Soviets rejected the second draft because of the on-site inspections, and the first because it was not comprehensive.

In early November, the Soviets hinted that they could adopt a proposal developed by three American and three Soviet scientists which called for unmanned, automatic recording stations as control monitors, plus a small number of on-site investigations. Disagreement immediately centered on the number of such "black boxes," the United States minimum being ten, the Soviet maximum being three.

The reception of this proposal in Congress at the beginning of 1963 was not encouraging; a number of senators and representatives asked for a return to the 1958 "Geneva System" (twenty inspections and nineteen control stations), and even long-time pro-treaty Senator Humphrey warned United States negotiators that the Senate would never accept the Soviet proposal.

Alton Frye writes:

> One of the most vocal critics of the test ban discussion had been Senator Thomas J. Dodd. . . . But, in the spring of 1963, a series of private exchanges between Dodd and the United States Arms Control and Disarmament Agency persuaded the Senator that it was indeed possible to determine unilaterally whether another country was conducting tests in any environment except underground. This led Dodd to join Senator Hubert Humphrey and thirty-two co-sponsors in submitting a Senate resolution calling for a limited test ban.[54]

The proposal, on May 27, 1963, was that the United States offer at the upcoming high-level Moscow talks an accord banning tests in the atmosphere and underwater, to be monitored by national systems

54. Alton Frye, "Congress: The Virtues of Its Vices," *Foreign Policy* 3 (Summer 1971): 112–113.

with no on-site inspections. The Committee of Principals, expanded to include the Joint Chiefs in order to allay congressional criticism, recommended, however, that the United States press for a comprehensive test ban treaty.

By the end of the second day of negotiations in Moscow, however, it was clear that no agreement on a comprehensive test ban would be possible, given Soviet objections to on-site inspections. AEC Chairman Glenn Seaborg says:

> The Soviets were persuaded that the United States wanted to inspect in order to spy; many on our side were convinced that without adequate inspection the Soviets would cheat.[55]

In less than two weeks, however, a more limited treaty, containing much language originally proposed by United States negotiators in Geneva the year before, and prohibiting nuclear testing in the atmosphere, in outer space, and under water was concluded.[56]

Senate Foreign Relations Committee hearings on the treaty itself ran from August 8 to 27, and the Senate Preparedness Investigating Subcommittee of the Senate Armed Services Committee continued to hold hearings on general United States nuclear test ban policy during the same period. Administration testimony before the two committees was heavily favorable; the Joint Chiefs conceded that the benefits warranted acceptance of some military risks. Edward Teller and Dr. John Foster, director of the Lawrence Radiation Laboratory at Livermore, opposed the ban strongly and urged continued research through atmospheric testing, a position which they had always taken on any ban. Former participants in United States nuclear policy—Harold Stassen, Arthur Dean, John McCloy, and Linus Pauling—generally supported the treaty; opposition came from former Joint Chiefs and former AEC members.

The two committees heard somewhat different testimony. Witnesses before the Foreign Relations Committee were more concerned with international political implications of the treaty, and even the ostensibly "military" figures who appeared there could also

55. Seaborg, *Kennedy*, p. 242.
56. Seaborg, *Kennedy*, pp. 241–254. See also Arthur H. Dean, *Test Ban and Disarmament: The Path of Negotiation* (New York: Harper and Row, 1966), pp. 97–102; and Ronald J. Terchek, *The Making of the Test Ban Treaty* (The Hague: Martinus Nijhoff, 1970), p. 22.

be classified as political, while witnesses before the Preparedness Subcommittee were mostly professional military figures. This reflected the different ideological orientations of committee members, Senator John Stennis of the Armed Services Committee and his colleagues being more conservative than Senator J. William Fulbright and his associates, and led to two divergent reports on the treaty. On September 3, the Foreign Relations Committee reported the treaty favorably by a sixteen-to-one vote. Six days later, the Preparedness Investigating Subcommittee voted five to two that the treaty would result in serious, and perhaps insurmountable, military and technical disadvantages.

President Kennedy worked with great dedication to achieve a strong Senate ratification. He met individually with senators and sent letters to Senate leaders Mansfield and Dirksen on September 11 to allay any fears they had about test continuation, United States diligence in checking Soviet adherence to the treaty, or our other military capabilities. To support the President's assurances, two underground tests were conducted in Nevada two days later. Kennedy considered creation of a Citizens Committee for a Nuclear Test Ban to provide grass-roots pressure on Congress, but this proved unnecessary; the Senate ratified the treaty by eighty to nineteen on September 24. On October 7, 1963, President Kennedy signed the treaty.

These three cases differ significantly in a number of particulars. Consider the time span covered by each:

1. Civilian Control of Atomic Energy
   First Proposed: Bush-Conant Bill, 1944
   Final Enactment: AEC Bill, 1946
   Elapsed Time: Two years

2. National Science Foundation
   First Proposed: Bush, *Science, the Endless Frontier*, 1945
   Final Enactment: NSF Bill, 1950
   Elapsed Time: Five years

3. Test Ban
   First Proposed: Acheson-Lilienthal Plan, 1946
   Final Enactment: Test Ban Treaty, 1963
   Elapsed Time: Seventeen years

Differences in elapsed time reflect differences in the complexity of the task faced by those having the responsibility or harboring the desire to innovate, in creating consensus among decision-makers' perceptions of "needs" and their consequent readiness to come to an agreement to act. Perhaps the most noteworthy feature of the test ban case is not the difficulty United States negotiators experienced in finding common ground with the USSR, but rather the difficulty proponents of the test ban had in getting agreement within the American government on the desirability of a treaty. The problem turned on two issues: the reliance for budgetary reasons during the Eisenhower administration on the strategic doctrine of "massive retaliation," which created bureaucratic obligations among those responsible for the nation's strategic posture to argue for flexibility in the maintenance and improvement of American atomic capability, and the vexing technical problem of detection. Only toward the end of the seventeen years did beliefs about the feasibility of detection find a foundation in technical knowledge independent of beliefs about the desirability of a test ban treaty. Thus the research that went into detection measures can be identified as having had a powerful independent role in facilitating United States acquiescence to a test ban.

It seems likely that the longer the process of innovation, the more significant will be the fundamental intellectual tasks of identifying the empirical premises of policy alternatives and finding means to support or refute them by recourse to evidence. Fast policy initiation needs little empirical back-up; more or less spontaneous agreement makes it unnecessary. Slow policy initiation entails not only more evidence and more knowledge but also the search for appropriate forums in which evidence can be marshalled and publicized.

III

Foreign Policy Innovation

Innovations in policy that happen fairly rapidly, I have suggested, seem likely to have in common the fact that major participants in the development are more or less in agreement about the nature of the problem to be faced, even when they do not agree about the desirability of various proposed solutions. Differences in the internal environments within different governmental agencies give different actors different interests to protect, but common exposure to the subculture of high policymaking should help them to see problems in ways sufficiently alike that they are able to communicate with one another, propose competing solutions, and implement decisions once made.

Perhaps the most significant American policy innovation in foreign affairs since World War II was facilitated by an influential subcultural framework. The decision to give substantial aid to Greece and Turkey in the immediate postwar era has been reexamined by revisionist historians in the light of their latter-day beliefs about opportunities that then existed for peaceful coexistence with the Soviet Union and their sharply revised assessments of threats to world peace posed by the various great powers.[1] It will not serve my purposes to comment

1. See William Appleman Williams, *The Tragedy of American Diplomacy*, rev. ed. (New York: Dell, 1962); D. F. Fleming, *The Cold War and its Origins* (Garden City, N.Y.: Doubleday, 1961); Gar Alperovitz, *Atomic Diplomacy* (New York: Simon and Schuster, 1965); David Horowitz, *Containment and Revolution* (Boston: Beacon Press, 1967); Gabriel Kolko, *The Roots of American Foreign Policy* (Boston: Beacon Press, 1969); Barton Bernstein, ed., *Politics and Policies of the Truman Administration* (Chicago: Quadrangle Books, 1970); and Lloyd C. Gardner, *Architects of Illusion* (Chicago: Quadrangle Books, 1970). For other viewpoints, see Paul Seabury, *The Rise and Decline of the Cold War* (New York: Basic Books, 1967); H. Stuart Hughes, "The Second Year of the Cold War," *Commentary* 48 (August 1969): 27–32; Robert James Maddox, *The New Left and the Origins of the Cold War* (Princeton, N.J.: Princeton University Press, 1973); and Thomas T. Hammond, ed., *Witnesses to the Origins of the Cold War* (Seattle: University of Washington Press, 1982).

on the substance of the revisionist argument, except to acknowledge that one premise upon which it is built, namely, the existence of a subculture of decision-makers who rapidly came to see the central issues in much the same way, seems well-founded.

Indeed, so well-founded is this belief that it leads to two further considerations. First, we must ask if a strong consensus among policymakers about problem-definition leads to a condition that one social scientist (presumably following Orwell) has named "group-think";[2] and second, we must consider whether or under what conditions, if ever, such a consensus is a necessary condition of any sort of policy innovation at all.

Groupthink is a label that has been attached to processes producing decisions that turned out badly (at least from the perspective of the psychologist giving the account), and in which alternative courses of action were sooner or later rejected. The processes by which alternatives are winnowed away—group processes that might in another context be interpreted as necessary for the formation of a collective judgment strong enough to support any action at all, and that have as their object the rejection of alternatives and the channelling of group energy, resources, and attention toward a limited set of options—are given an unfavorable description. The question is whether "consensus formation," a less pejorative label for these processes, is normally distinguishable from "groupthink" while the process is going on and without the enlightenment available to those who know how things turned out.

If observers disagree about outcomes, they may well reach opposite conclusions about the appropriateness of the processes that produced those outcomes. One of the commonest complaints that appears in the annals of national decision-making, as was pointed out in the discussion of the Eisenhower administration's approach to the test ban treaty, is that decision-makers refused to listen or were prevented from listening to a point of view espoused by the complainant. To the outsider, however, this situation is frequently indistinguishable from the situation in which the decision-maker is perfectly well aware of the complaint but for one reason or another chooses to reject it.[3] The actual basis of the complaint may be that for one reason or another the complainant is sympathetic to the losing side of a battle within the government.

If the alternative that won the internal governmental battle works out badly, the supposition is that it could not possibly have prevailed on its merits and that therefore something was wrong with the process that permitted it to emerge. This is, however, a shaky proposition at best, since rejected alternatives might well have been worse.[4] If history is written by advocates of one or another alternative not chosen, there is a risk that a fair-minded reconstruction of the real decision-making climate will prove to be difficult. Instead, an account of decision-making may be reduced to the level of the famous Dogpatch beauty contest, in which after seeing the first finalist the judges awarded the prize to the other contestant, sight unseen.[5]

Neither of our foreign policy innovations is by common opinion considered a fiasco, however, so evidence of "groupthink" is hard to pin down. Consensus formation, however, in the case of the Truman Doctrine, is of overwhelming importance in enabling innovation.[6]

3. For a much more optimistic view of the possibilities, see Alexander L. George, "The Case for Multiple Advocacy in Making Foreign Policy," *American Political Science Review* 66 (September 1972): 751–785.

4. Readers who are interested in pursuit of this problem can find considerable food for thought by examining Leslie H. Gelb and Richard Betts, *The Irony of Vietnam: The System Worked* (Washington, D.C.: Brookings Institution, 1979).

5. I am tempted to make this criticism of Janis's discussion of Vietnam escalation, (*Groupthink*, pp. 101–135) in light of the memoirs of George Ball and John Kenneth Galbraith. Ball says:

I was irked when some academic writers . . . implied that my long-sustained effort to extricate us from Vietnam was merely a stylized exercise by an in-house devil s advocate.

George W. Ball, *The Past Has Another Pattern* (New York: Norton, 1982), p. 384. Galbraith says:

Throughout the whole Vietnam controversy the three men to whom those of us opposing the war had access were George Ball, the accepted inside opponent, McGeorge Bundy and [Robert] McNamara. These men, later much criticized, had the gratitude of those of us on whom they did not slam the door.

John Kenneth Galbraith, *A Life in Our Times* (New York: Ballantine, 1981), p. 471. The issue is by no means a simple one and deserves further discussion.

6. On the general problem see McGeorge Bundy, *The Strength of Government* (Cambridge: Harvard University Press, 1968).

1. THE TRUMAN DOCTRINE: AID TO GREECE AND TURKEY

In 1947 world events and the opinions of domestic policymakers were by no means acting in concert to present a clear and certain description of the United States' future role in Europe. However, during that year the United States would extend large amounts of aid to Europe, adopt a policy of attempting to contain what were believed to be expansionist Soviet pressures, and participate in the beginnings of the cold war.[7]

Events in the international environment stimulated continued American involvement in postwar world affairs, a situation never before faced by peacetime American leaders. Immediate pressures centered around the withdrawal of the British military presence from the eastern Mediterranean and simultaneous internal crises facing Greece and Turkey, and it was in response to these stimuli that the Truman Doctrine was to be invented. Greece was near the brink of total economic and political collapse just after the war, and a Communist takeover was expected. The Greek economy had been demolished during the German occupation, with consequent postwar problems of inefficiency and corruption. The Greek government was threatened by approximately thirteen thousand well-trained and equipped Communist guerrilla troops who had found refuge in Yugoslavia, Bulgaria, and Albania. The Greek army was poorly trained and demoralized, and the guerrillas posed a sizable threat to the govern-

---

7. As is true of most published historical discussions of this period, the present treatment relies heavily on the eyewitness account of United States decision-making contained in Joseph M. Jones, *The Fifteen Weeks: February 21–June 5, 1947* (New York: Viking, 1955). See Richard J. Barnet, *Intervention and Revolution* (New York: New American Library, 1968), pp. 97–131, who in a revisionist history says that the Jones book

contains many quotations from draft documents at the time, which have not yet been made public in any other source. The accuracy of his account is attested to by George Kennan, who was director of the Policy Planning Staff at the time . . . [saying] "Mr. Joseph Jones, in his excellent book, *The Fifteen Weeks*, has described in great and faithful detail the various discussions, consultations, clearances, and literary struggles that took place within the government . . . " and by Louis Halle, another member of [the policy planning] staff (p. 128).

ment.[8] The army had received financial support and, in 1944, sixteen thousand troops from Britain. While the latter did much to stabilize the situation in Athens, British troops did not engage in fighting the guerrillas.[9]

Turkey was in less immediate danger. While faced with many economic problems, it had maintained a sound agrarian economic base. Nor did it have the insurgency problem that threatened Greece. Rather, Turkey's main threat was external. In 1945 the Soviet Union had announced the annulment of a twenty-year-old neutrality treaty and demanded the cession of certain Turkish districts on the Turkish-Soviet border. Communist newspapers argued that Turkey had no right to exist. Twenty-five motorized Soviet divisions were placed close to the Russo-Turkish border.[10] Turkish ability to respond to these threats was limited by the state of its army of six hundred thousand troops, a force so ill-equipped that Secretary of War Robert S. Patterson was later to describe it as "a 1910 army."[11] Even this level of military mobilization placed so great a strain on Turkey's economy that the country was threatened with bankruptcy. The fate of Turkey was regarded as linked to the outcome in Greece. If Greece fell to the Communists, Turkey would be encircled, and most officials in the West thought it would also succumb to Soviet domination.[12]

Although the international scene was becoming more and more troublesome, it was by no means certain that the United States would intervene. For the first time in fourteen years Congress was controlled by the relatively isolationist and fiscally conservative Republican party. Republican Senate leader Robert A. Taft of Ohio had promised during the 1946 congressional campaign that the Truman budget would be cut significantly so as to be brought into balance. Sentiment also ran high in that election to dismantle wartime controls on the domestic economy and "bring the boys home." In 1945 a

8. See Jones, *Fifteen Weeks*, p. 25; and Dean Acheson, *Present at the Creation* (New York: Norton, 1969), p. 219.

9. Jones, *Fifteen Weeks*, p. 27.

10. Ibid., p. 61.

11. Walter Millis, ed., *The Forrestal Diaries* (New York: Viking, 1957), p. 257.

12. Ibid.; Cabell Phillips, *The Truman Presidency* (Baltimore: Penguin Books, 1966), p. 168.

majority of Republican congressmen had voted against the creation of the International Monetary Fund. With a Republican majority in Congress after 1946, the support and assistance of several prominent Republicans, including Senate Foreign Relations Committee chairman Arthur Vandenberg, were required to obtain passage of even a limited trade agreement program allowing partial tariff reductions.[13] The Republicans had supported creation of the United Nations in the hope that the United States would be allowed to recede from world embroilments.[14] Thus, in late February 1947, when First Secretary of the British Embassy H. M. Sichel delivered to Loy Henderson, the State Department's Director of the Office of Near Eastern and African Affairs, a memorandum informing the United States of Britain's imminent decision to pull out of Greece and Turkey, it was far from obvious that the United States would assume the burden of making up for British influence in the area.

The United States—and particularly the State Department—wanted and expected Britain to take the lead in countering Soviet efforts in the Middle East and the Mediterranean. Secretary of the Navy James Forrestal recorded in his diary in 1946 that he had asked Undersecretary of State Acheson about United States policy in Turkey. Acheson had replied that the British should furnish Turkey with the necessary arms. In the event that Britain was not capable of providing suitable armaments, the United States would give Britain the arms needed to make sufficient transfers.[15] Further evidence of this approach is apparent in a scholarly examination of the congressional discussion surrounding economic aid legislation for Britain in 1946:

> Some case can be made to suggest that the loan of 3.25 billion dollars to Britain in 1946 was to be used to shore up the British and enable them to continue to check Soviet penetration in the Mediterranean and the

13. This had been the keystone of Secretary of State Hull's foreign policy throughout the 1930s. Acheson, *Creation*, pp. 9–10.

14. David S. McLellan and John W. Reuss, "Foreign and Military Policies," in Richard S. Kirkendall, ed., *The Truman Period as a Research Field* (Columbia, Mo.: University of Missouri Press, 1967), p. 56.

15. Millis, ed., *Forrestal*, p. 216.

Middle East. Even if this were not the rationale for the loan among the leaders of the Administration, it certainly became the dominant theme when the enabling legislation reached the Congress. The traditional Anglophobes in the Congress accused the Administration of attempting to "pull British chestnuts out of the fire." As the debate proceeded and the outcome hung in the balance, the arguments shifted rather abruptly. At first supported for economic reasons, the debate over the loan ended on a distinctly political and security note. Finally, the loan was supported because it would allow the British to uphold the security and integrity of their sphere of influence. The Congress seemed to be saying that, regardless of how distasteful British imperialism might be, it was better for us to pay them to watch the Russians than to do it ourselves.[16]

In 1946, however, the United States did become directly involved in the Greek crisis and began to consider a direct response. The Greek government had repeatedly asked the United States to increase its limited financial aid. Under existing appropriations and authority little more could be done. With no reasonable assurance of repayment, the Export-Import Bank was not authorized to make Greece a loan. President Truman, after conversing with Undersecretaries of State Dean Acheson and William Clayton, had become convinced that the Greek economy and administrative system were in complete chaos. In 1947, Truman sent the American Economic Mission, headed by Paul A. Porter, a well-known Washington lawyer, to Greece to investigate the situation. Porter coordinated his work with the United States representative on the United Nations' commission to investigate Greek frontier incidents, Mark Ethridge, the distinguished editor and publisher of the *Louisville Courier-Journal*, and with the American Ambassador in Athens, Lincoln MacVeagh, in examining the Greek political and economic situation. By late February the combined judgment of these three observers was that British troop withdrawals were imminent, and that unless the Greek government received immediate assurance of large-scale military and financial aid from the United States, it would crumble within a matter of weeks. The way would then be open for a successful Communist takeover.[17] They also argued that the aid would have to

16. McLellan and Reuss, "Foreign and Military Policies," pp. 54–55.
17. Acheson, *Creation*, p. 217.

be administered by an American mission in order to bring about a reorganization of the Greek economy and administrative system. This information was received by Undersecretary Acheson and passed on to Secretary of State George Marshall in a memorandum entitled "Crisis and the Imminent Possibility of Collapse" on February 20. "All signs," wrote Acheson, "point to an impending move by the communists to take over the country." The next day Acheson learned that the rumored British pullout from the Mediterranean area was indeed "imminent"—that an official declaration of British policy on this matter would be given to Secretary Marshall on Monday, February 24, notifying the American government that British aid to the Greek and Turkish governments would end in six weeks' time.[18]

The British had planned to withdraw half of their troops immediately and the other half before March 31. Britain, deep in economic trouble, was relinquishing its costly position as a world power. Later, during Senate hearings, Senator Walter George of the Foreign Relations Committee would express strong criticism of Britain for presenting the Greek-Turkish problem to the United States as a crisis, with little warning or time for deliberation and transition of responsibilities.[19]

> Could it be possible, for instance, that the British felt they had to act precipitately in order to force the United States to respond forcefully to the Communist threat in the Balkans, that, otherwise, the United States, judging by its record up to that time, might not act successfully, responsibly, or perhaps at all?[20]

The same day that Acheson learned of the proposed British action (Friday, February 21) he called for a series of reports to be made ready from the Near Eastern and European divisions of the State Department on four questions:

1. the facts of the situation as seen by the United States representatives in the area;

---

18. Ibid.
19. Millis, ed., *Forrestal*, p. 261.
20. McLellan and Reuss, "Foreign and Military Policies," pp. 55–56.

2. the amounts of money and personnel that could be made available on relatively short notice;
3. the amounts of money and personnel that would be required to stabilize the situation in Greece and Turkey; and
4. a more general statement on the importance of an independent Greece and Turkey to the future existence of western Europe.

The next two days were spent in the preparation and revision of these reports. The tenor of the papers and the attitudes of the participants toward the situation at hand is revealingly described by Acheson:

> Henderson asked me whether we were still working on papers bearing on the making of a decision or the execution of one. I said the latter; under the circumstances there could be only one decision. At that we drank a martini or two toward the confusion of our enemies.[21]

On Sunday afternoon, February 23, Henderson delivered the final draft of the papers to Acheson.[22] The following day Acheson presided over a conference attended by Henderson, Assistant Secretary John Hickerson, Secretary of War Robert Patterson, and Secretary of the Navy Forrestal. Here the international implications of aid to Greece and Turkey were considered. Joseph Jones, then a member of the State Department public affairs staff and author of an enthusiastic "inside" book depicting the events leading to the establishment of the Truman Doctrine, reports the conference's agreement:

> At the time Acheson summed up the conclusions, and all found themselves in agreement that it was vital to the security of the United States that Greece and Turkey be strengthened; that only the United States was in a position to do this; and that the President should therefore ask Congress for necessary funds and authority.[23]

At a meeting with the Department's political, economic, legal, and information officers on Tuesday, February 25, Acheson laid out the problem posed by Britain's withdrawal from Greece and Turkey and proposed several courses of action the United States might consider.

21. Acheson, *Creation*, p. 218.
22. Jones, *Fifteen Weeks*, p. 134.
23. Ibid., p. 135.

There was a free exchange of ideas, but a general consensus was formed that it was vital to United States security that Greece and Turkey remain outside the Soviet sphere of influence. After the meeting, Acheson, Henderson, and the Near Eastern Affairs staff drafted the State Department's final statement, entitled "Positions and Recommendations of the Department of State Regarding Immediate Aid to Greece and Turkey." In addition to stating the general position that the political and territorial integrity of Turkey and Greece should be maintained and that the United States should extend aid necessary to assure their democratic development, this paper contained specific recommendations proposing (1) that legislation be put forward for long-range financial aid and also to authorize the Export-Import Bank to extend credits free from normal restrictions; (2) that all available military supplies be transferred to Greece and Turkey and that Congress be presented with legislation authorizing additional military supplies and equipment; (3) that Congress be asked to send United States government personnel for administrative, economic, and financial work with the Greek government; (4) that plans be worked out for an American administrative organization in Greece to control the use of funds and supplies provided by the United States; (5) that discussions be begun with the British representative in Washington on Greece's military needs and ways of fulfilling them; and (6) that the public be informed of the urgent need of aid to Greece.[24]

The statement was presented to Secretaries of the Navy and War Forrestal and Patterson by Secretary of State Marshall and Undersecretary Acheson on February 26. Earlier, Army Chief of Staff Dwight D. Eisenhower in a memorandum to Patterson had called attention to the problem of foreign aid and suggested a study be made of the needs of all foreign countries that might need United States aid. At the meeting Eisenhower's memorandum was discussed. Recognizing that such a study would take a long time to prepare and that the Greek crisis required immediate action, they agreed that any decision on Greece could not wait. Consequently Forrestal and Patterson endorsed the State Department's positions and recommendations. However, it was understood that a study would be made

24. Ibid., pp. 136–137.

of the aid requirements of other countries in the future.

That afternoon Marshall and Acheson met with President Truman and explained the joint recommendations of the Departments of State, War, and the Navy. Well-versed in the problem, Truman needed little briefing or convincing that the situation demanded a major United States commitment. He was more concerned with obtaining congressional authorization. To this end he decided to invite various congressional leaders to the White House the next day to hear Marshall and Acheson present the proposed program and to solicit their reactions. At that meeting, the floor leaders of both parties in the House and Senate and the chairmen and ranking minority members of the House and Senate Foreign Relations and Appropriations Committees were all in attendance.

Secretary Marshall began the White House meeting with the presentation of the problem the United States faced in regard to British withdrawal of economic support from Turkey and Greece. Hearing Marshall advise United States support primarily on humanitarian grounds, Acheson became apprehensive that the senators were not seeing the seriousness of the situation in terms of United States security. Acheson writes:

> These congressmen had no conception of what challenged them; it was my task to bring it home. Both my superiors, equally perturbed, gave me the floor. . . . No time was left for measured appraisal. In the past eighteen months, I said, Soviet pressure on the Straits, on Iran, and on northern Greece had brought the Balkans to the point where a highly possible Soviet breakthrough might open three continents to Soviet penetration. Like apples in a barrel infected by one rotten one, the corruption of Greece would infect Iran and all to the east. It would also carry infection to Africa through Asia Minor and Egypt, and to Europe through Italy and France, already threatened by the strongest domestic Communist parties in Western Europe. The Soviet Union was playing one of the greatest gambles in history at minimal cost. It did not need to win all the possibilities. Even one or two offered immense gains. We and we alone were in a position to break up the play. These were the stakes that British withdrawal from the eastern Mediterranean offered to an eager and ruthless opponent.[25]

---

25. Acheson, *Creation*, p. 219; Jones, *Fifteen Weeks*, p. 141. An argument similar to this one made in connection with United States policy toward southeast Asia twenty

Senator Vandenberg commented after Acheson finished that the country was faced with a serious situation, of which aid to these two countries was only a part. He felt it imperative that any request for aid to Greece and Turkey be accompanied by a message to Congress and an explanation to the American people of the grim facts of the larger threat to which he and the others had been listening. Vandenberg advised the President, "If that's what you want, there's only one way to get it. That is to make a personal appearance before Congress and scare hell out of the country."[26] While there were no definite commitments made among those at the meeting, neither was there serious opposition. Senator Taft had asserted that the United States was being tricked into bailing the British out, but Vandenberg and the others saw the crisis as an example of a worldwide ideological clash between East and West.[27] Jones records that the impression was gained by administration officials that these congressional leaders would support measures to aid Greece and Turkey if Vandenberg's "conditions" of messages to Congress and to the public were met. Before the meeting ended, Truman promised to deliver a detailed program and the statements Vandenberg had requested.

The State Department was charged with drafting the messages, the content of which followed closely the recommendations developed during the week of February 21–28.[28] The draft was considered and revised at three separate conferences. Cleared by Marshall, it

---

years later has been described as a "domino theory" and derided as simpleminded. As Janis says:

> Johnson's inner circle uncritically accepted the domino theory, which simplistically assumes that all Asian countries will act alike, so that if the Communists were permitted to gain control over one country in the Far East, all neighboring countries would promptly become vulnerable and fall under Communist domination.

Janis, *Groupthink*, p. 116. Whether either of these estimates was actually simpleminded depends on the empirical bases for making them. In the present case we can say that it is a historical fact that Undersecretary Acheson's argument persuaded those who heard it.

26. Eric F. Goldman, *The Crucial Decade* (New York: Vintage, 1960), p. 59.
27. Phillips, *Truman Presidency*, p. 175.
28. Jones, *Fifteen Weeks*, pp. 148–149.

was sent to the President's adviser on state messages, Clark Clifford, where it received primarily stylistic changes.

While the President's message was being prepared, Acheson held talks with press representatives in an effort to prepare the public for a major policy change. The *New York Times* on March 8 reported a "growing excitement on Capitol Hill with a generally favorable sentiment apparent."[29] Jones observes that these conferences had great utility:

> A great deal of the radio, editorial, and columnist comment during the early days of March . . . encouraged those engaged in articulating and implementing policy and performed an invaluable service as advance agent to Congress and the public for the President's message of March 12.[30]

On March 1, the British ambassador, Lord Inverchapel, called on Acheson to learn of United States intentions in Greece and Turkey. Acheson assured him that the United States would soon act and requested that the British not pull out before United States efforts could be initiated. Several days later Inverchapel notified Acheson of Britain's willingness to cooperate, noting that they would not withdraw all their troops before the summer.

On March 7, President Truman called a cabinet meeting to discuss the Greek-Turkish crisis and the appropriate United States response. At the beginning of the meeting President Truman stated that the decision he faced concerning the Greece-Turkey crisis was the most serious that he had confronted while President and that he wanted a full cabinet discussion of the problem. He then had Undersecretary Acheson describe the situation. There was a consensus among those attending that Greece should be supported to the fullest extent possible.[31] While there was general agreement with the plan that had been developed, several were dubious that Congress would approve the measures.

Secretary Forrestal suggested that the government obtain the assistance of businessmen, who, he argued, could play an important

29. Ibid., p. 163; Acheson, *Creation*, p. 220.
30. Jones, *Fifteen Weeks*, p. 145.
31. Millis, ed., *Forrestal*, p. 251; Acheson, *Creation*, p. 221.

role in improving the Greek economy. At the conclusion of the discussion President Truman appointed a committee headed by Secretary of the Treasury John Snyder, Secretary of Commerce Averell Harriman, Patterson, Forrestal, and Acheson to form a program for communicating with leaders throughout the country and especially with a select group of business leaders. At the committee's first meeting (the next day) it was decided to send working groups comprised of experts in government, communications, transportation, and so forth, to Greece.[32]

Three days later Truman again invited congressional leaders to the White House for a conference on the Greek crisis. Truman explained the situation and the administration's proposal for dealing with it. There was considerable discussion, but no opposition was registered. After the meeting Senator Vandenberg called a meeting of Republican legislators and briefed them on the President's forthcoming message to Congress. He said he would reserve judgment until after the message was delivered, but emphasized that this was a national policy of the highest order and that it had nothing to do with partisan politics.[33]

On March 12, President Truman addressed a joint session of Congress where the "Truman Doctrine" was clearly enunciated for the first time. "I believe," said the President, "that it must be the policy of the United States to support free peoples who are resisting attempted subjugation by armed minorities or by outside pressures. I believe that we must assist free peoples to work out their own destinies in their own way." The President asked Congress to appropriate $250 million in military and economic aid to Greece and $150 million in aid to Turkey, toward the achievement of these goals. He additionally sought authority to send both civilian and military missions to the two countries to oversee the operations of the programs and to assist in restructuring their governments, economies, and armed forces. Pointing to British intentions to withdraw in late March, he asked for the legislation by March 31.[34]

Reaction to the President's message was immediate. The next day

32. Millis, ed., *Forrestal*, p. 252.
33. Jones, *Fifteen Weeks*, pp. 188–189.
34. Acheson, *Creation*, p. 222; Phillips, *Truman Presidency*, p. 176.

Senator Vandenberg, at a meeting of the Republican Policy Conference attended by all fifty-two Republican senators, endorsed the Truman proposal. However, Senator Taft, fearful of a war with Russia, expressed opposition to sending military missions to those countries.

The most virulent attack came from Truman's former Secretary of Commerce, Henry Wallace. In a radio broadcast, Wallace accused the President of being "the best salesman communism ever had," and of plunging the world into a "century of fear."[35] Opposition was great among both strong isolationists and internationalists; they found themselves united in complaining that the administration had ignored the United Nations. While other issues, such as support of a reactionary and corrupt Greek regime, high costs, and the way Congress had been handed a "crisis" with a request for immediate approval, engendered criticism, the bypassing of the United Nations was the most unpopular aspect of the administration's handling of the issue with both Congress and the press.[36] Even supporters of the legislation regretted the administration's oversight. Senator Vandenberg would later write, "The administration made a colossal blunder in ignoring the United Nations."[37]

On March 20, Senator Vandenberg and Tom Connally, the ranking Democrat on the Senate Foreign Relations Committee, consulting closely with Acheson and other congressmen, introduced a lengthy amendment stating that United States aid to Greece and Turkey was necessary because the United Nations was not yet able to furnish the assistance required, and that the United States was contributing to the freedom and independence of all members of the United Nations in accord with the principles of the United Nations charter. To further mollify the opposition on the United Nations issue, Warren R. Austin, the United States representative, made a statement to the Security Council on March 28 in which he suggested that United Nations action in Greece and United States emergency aid were

---

35. Jones, *Fifteen Weeks*, p. 187.

36. See Lawrence S. Wittner, *American Intervention In Greece, 1943–1949* (New York: Columbia University Press, 1982), pp. 79–94, for a generally sympathetic canvass of opposition views.

37. Arthur H. Vandenberg, Jr., ed., *The Private Papers of Senator Vandenberg* (Boston: Houghton Mifflin, 1952), p. 345.

complementary. Austin also assured the Council that the United States wanted the United Nations to take over the whole job in Greece as soon as possible. The United Nations issue was largely eliminated from debate when several days later another amendment by Senator Vandenberg was introduced which instructed the President to withdraw aid if (1) the governments or a majority of the people of such a nation requested him to; (2) the United States was officially notified that assistance furnished by the United Nations made United States aid unnecessary; or (3) the President found that the purposes of the Act had been accomplished by other intergovernmental organizations or were incapable of satisfactory accomplishment.[38]

Hearings of the Senate Committee on Foreign Relations began on March 24 and continued through March 31. The House Committee on Foreign Affairs hearings began on March 20 and lasted until April 10. Principal government witnesses before both Committees included Acheson, Patterson, Forrestal, Clayton, and Paul Porter.

It is worth underscoring the extent to which congressional hearings play a part in the policy initiation process even when, as in this case, members of Congress are not prime movers. Here they are supplying the arena through which a policy already decided upon can be given public legitimacy. Vandenberg was explicit in acknowledging this role when he stipulated that President Truman "scare hell out of the country" as a condition of his support.

The Senate Committee unanimously approved the bill with the Vandenberg amendment and reported it out of committee on April 3. On the floor, Democratic Senators Claude Pepper of Florida and Glen Taylor of Idaho argued that United States aid should be funnelled through the United Nations. Republican Senators Kenneth Wherry of Nebraska, George Malone of Nevada, and Wayland Brooks of Illinois argued that the program would lead to war or bankruptcy. It was passed on April 22 by a vote of 67 to 23, receiving sub-

---

38. Jones, *Fifteen Weeks*, p. 189. Acheson writes that "this, of course, was window dressing and must have seemed silly or cynical or both in London, Paris and Moscow." He argues that minor nit-picking such as this was the price that the administration had to pay for the support of Senator Vandenberg, who used such minor issues as a stratagem for obtaining Republican support on foreign policy matters (pp. 223–224).

stantial bipartisan support, with 32 Democrats and 35 Republicans voting approval and 7 Democrats and 16 Republicans opposed. "For the administration," Lawrence Wittner says, "it was a hard-fought and important victory."[39] The bill was reported favorably out of the House Foreign Affairs Committee on April 25 and, after three days of debate, was approved 287 to 107. Minor differences required that the measures go to conference; the conference report was accepted by voice votes in both houses.

Many congressmen expressed displeasure at being given so little time properly to consider aid to Greece and Turkey and its broader implications. Senator Vandenberg, in a private letter written on the same day Senate hearings began, expressed Congress's dilemma:

> The trouble is that these "crises" never reach Congress until they have developed to a point where Congressional discretion is pathetically restricted. When things finally reach a point where a President asks us to "declare war" there usually is nothing left except to "declare war." In the present instance, the overriding fact is that the President had made a long-delayed statement regarding Communism on-the-march which must be supported if there is any hope of ever impressing Moscow with the necessity of paying any sort of peaceful attention to us whatever. If we turned the President down—after his speech to the joint Congressional session—we might as well either resign ourselves to a complete Communist encirclement and infiltration or else get ready for World War No. Three.[40]

On May 22, only two months after he formally requested it, President Truman signed the legislation.

2. THE FORMATION OF THE PEACE CORPS

The second case of foreign policy innovation is radically different from some of the cases that have been discussed so far. No set of urgent circumstances directly impinging upon the immediate short-

39. Wittner, *American Intervention in Greece*, p. 94.
40. Vandenberg, ed., *Private Papers*, letter of March 24, 1947, p. 342. Alert readers will note that the manufacture of a crisis restricting congressional options was more or less what Vandenberg had asked President Truman for at the February 27 meeting.

run interests of the United States, as perceived by its highest officials, created a "need" that the Peace Corps had to be invented to meet. There was—and is—certainly a need in the world for the type of work that the Peace Corps does, but the circumstances surrounding the transformation of this vague, chronic need into a policy innovation of the United States government show a process more like the later stages of the nuclear test ban than any of the other cases I have so far considered.

The central idea of the Peace Corps—government-sponsored contributions by Americans of their technical skills to projects abroad—has a long history that weaves together strands from disparate traditions: missionary work, volunteer work abroad, technical assistance, and national service for young people. Unlike missionary work, Peace Corps service involves host nations in defining the tasks of American volunteers. Unlike volunteer programs, the Peace Corps is a government enterprise. Unlike people providing government technical assistance, however, Corpsmen work under the direction of locals at nominal, not professional, wages. And unlike the draft, the Corps is neither compulsory nor subject to conventional military discipline or diplomatic corps controls.

Because of this hybrid background, while it is possible to identify the point at which the name "Peace Corps" was attached to the project, and it is even possible to say when a general Peace Corps-like idea was first introduced into the subculture of decision-makers, it is impossible to say where the idea originally came from. Peace Corps semiofficial literature traces the idea to the nineteenth-century American philosopher William James, who called for "conscription of our youthful population . . . to coal and iron mines, to freight trains . . . to dish washing"; James's goal, however, was supplanting the "war function," not providing foreign social service.[41]

Privately funded voluntary organizations contributed something of a model for the Peace Corps. One of the best known of these, and the one that attracted the attention of early Peace Corps supporter Hubert Humphrey, was the American Friends Service Committee

---

41. George Sullivan, *The Story of the Peace Corps* (New York: Fleet, 1964), p. 23.

(AFSC), which as long ago as 1919 dispatched teams of young people to serve in underprivileged areas. This work-camp concept was extended to overseas nations by the AFSC in 1960, and teams of young people were working in India and Tanganyika in that crucial summer when the Peace Corps was becoming a campaign issue.

The Experiment in International Living (EIL), founded in 1932, was responsible for the enthusiasm of the first Peace Corps director, Sargent Shriver, who had been a group leader for the Experiment in the 1930s, and that of Democratic Representative Henry Reuss of Wisconsin, an early Peace Corps backer in the House of Representatives, whose wife had been an Experimenter during that period. The EIL was aimed at bringing together groups of foreign nationals to share living experiences, not at providing development aid.

Operation Crossroads Africa, founded in 1957, was also aimed at "fostering communication"; its volunteers worked with their hosts on public improvement projects in African communities. President Kennedy later credited the small-scale Crossroads program with being the "progenitor of the Peace Corps."

The first government-connected program of this type was the International Volunteer Service. IVS was founded by an interdenominational religious group in 1953, in response to a plea by foreign aid officials for private support. IVS coordinated private technical assistance programs under government contract or private donation, and sent teams of young Americans into Laos, Vietnam, Egypt, and elsewhere, to teach agriculture and home economics.

The list of such private "progenitors" over the past half century could be greatly expanded. Most resembled the Peace Corps only in their concern for foreign development, for they were essentially financial assistance programs; those few that did feature volunteer teams of young people (e.g., Operation Crossroads Africa) did not have them actually living in a host community for any length of time, as part of its middle level of technicians.

The first advocacy of a Peace Corps-like government program was contained in an insignificant section of the 1950 United Auto Workers political platform, which proposed a program "where young American engineers, agricultural specialists, doctors, nurses, and teachers can use their energies, training, and creative ingenuity to assist and train the people of underdeveloped countries."[42] The UAW was to support later programs aimed at this goal, but there is no evidence that the 1950 proposal was noticed or elaborated by anyone.

In 1954, Heinz Rollman, a World War II German refugee and North Carolina businessman, wrote and published a book, *World Construction*,[43] in which he argued for a "Peace Army" of three million Americans, who would be sent to underdeveloped nations to help end disparities between them and the United States in areas like farming, housing, and industry. In his attempts to sell the idea, Rollman twice spoke about a "Peace Army" with President Eisenhower, but the idea failed to interest Eisenhower or congressional leaders. (In 1960, Eisenhower was to deride Kennedy's Peace Corps proposal as "warmed-over Rollman.")

In late 1957, Representative Henry Reuss suggested the idea of a "Youth Corps," to be part of the foreign aid program. He acknowledged the idea's kinship to the International Volunteer Service of the early 1950s, but said that his version came from observing American schoolteachers traveling from village to village in Cambodia to set up schools. Reuss did not immediately offer legislation on the subject, but he did find that the response to it at Cornell in a 1958 speech was "electric." A onetime Experiment in International Living leader, Sargent Shriver (then President of the Board of Education in Chicago) returned from his own tour of Asia that same year and presented a similar idea to President Eisenhower, who remained uninterested.

In January 1960, Congressman Reuss introduced a bill in the House requesting $10,000 to finance a study of the feasibility of his "Youth Corps" idea; Senator Richard Neuberger introduced an identical request in the Senate. As a foreign aid appropriation, Reuss's request went to the Foreign Operations Subcommittee of the House Appropriations Committee, where Representative Otto Passman (D-La.), an arch foe of the foreign aid bill, immediately struck out the $10,000 appropriation. Through sustained private argument, Reuss

42. Walter P. Reuther, *A Proposal for a Total Peace Offensive to Stop Communist Aggression by Taking the Initiative in the World Contest for Men's Minds, Hearts and Loyalties* (Detroit: International Union, United Automobile, Aircraft and Agricultural Implement Workers of America, CIO, 1950), p. 19.

43. Heinz Rollman, *World Construction* (New York: Greenberg Publishers, 1954).

got Passman to agree to go along with a conference report restoring the funds, if the Senate Appropriations Committee would do so. Senator Hubert Humphrey then made a similar and successful plea with Senator Carl Hayden, chairman of the Senate Appropriations Committee, and the funds were restored. The Foreign Operations Appropriations bill passed as a rider to the Mutual Security Act of 1960, and the research study was contracted by the State Department to the University of Colorado Research Foundation in June.

Senator Humphrey had long been impressed with the work of the American Friends Service Committee, and he, like Reuss, discovered from speaking to college groups in the late 1950s that the idea of a youth corps generated interest. Humphrey assigned his foreign relations adviser, Peter Grothe, to draft legislation, and on June 16, 1960, he introduced a bill calling for establishment of a "Peace Corps," to have five thousand volunteers in the field within five years. There was little chance for action on the bill because of the congressional adjournment schedule, but this was the first bill specifically intended to create this type of organization, as well as the first use of the name Peace Corps.

In September, Grothe took the proposal he had drafted to Archibald Cox, who was coordinating speech writing for presidential candidate John F. Kennedy. Vice-presidential candidate Lyndon Johnson used the Peace Corps idea in at least two speeches, and Kennedy foreign relations adviser Chester Bowles also tried it out several times. Senator Kennedy himself first proposed the Peace Corps in an extemporaneous talk during the campaign at the University of Michigan on October 14; like Reuss and Humphrey before him, Kennedy was struck by the students' response to his remarks, a feeling that was reinforced when he was presented with a petition expressing support for the idea, signed by several hundred University of Michigan students, while he was campaigning in Toledo several weeks later.[44]

Neither Kennedy nor his opponent, Vice-President Richard Nixon, made much of the Peace Corps as a campaign issue, however, and questions concerning it were far more often raised by audiences than

---

44. See Harris Wofford, *Of Kennedys and Kings* (New York: Farrar, Straus, Giroux, 1980), pp. 243–284.

initiated by the candidates' remarks. Kennedy finally delivered a major speech on the Peace Corps in San Francisco on November 2. This seems to have come about because Kennedy was impressed with student reaction. There were virtually no issues of any importance in the campaign, and it was rumored (incorrectly) that Nixon would soon endorse such a plan.

> Kennedy's timing reportedly caught the Nixon camp off base. The Vice-President's unenthusiastic treatment of such ideas disgruntled many Rockefeller Republicans who still considered the liberal Governor of New York their party's best bet. An advisor on African affairs testifies that in the early stages of the campaign he gave Nixon a study outlining a youth corps, but, as it turned out later, the plan was shelved. In the meantime, Robert Bowie, policy planning chief under the late Secretary of State Dulles, urged a Senate subcommittee to enlist 1,000 college graduates a year in a Foreign Service junior technical assistance corps. Later President Eisenhower's Committee on Information Activities Abroad suggested a similar long-term overseas youth aid program. A close aide to the former President said that the proposal was brought up at White House conferences and vetoed, mainly on objection from the Pentagon; he added, however, that both Eisenhower and Nixon spiritually liked the concept, but the grave reservations they had for its success overruled their sympathies. [45]

In his San Francisco proposal, Kennedy broadened the Peace Corps to include women and expanded the age specifications to avoid making it solely a "youth corps"; he also suggested that it be an "alternative to peace-time selective service," but this met a great deal of criticism and disappeared in all later statements.

Shortly after the election, President Kennedy set up a task force under his brother-in-law Sargent Shriver, who was then still in private business, to develop the idea of a Peace Corps. Dr. Max Millikin, director of the Center for International Studies at the Massachusetts Institute of Technology and a member of the task force, contributed a memo setting forth the need for skilled people in underdeveloped nations, as well as ways for young people to fill this demand.

45. Charles E. Wingenbach, *The Peace Corps—Who, How, and Where* (New York: John Day, 1963), pp. 26–27.

The principles set forth in this memorandum—that the Peace Corps should be a semi-autonomous agency; that the standards of selection should be maintained at a high level; that volunteers should serve in an operational (not advisory) capacity—came to be Peace Corps policy.[46]

Dr. Samuel Hayes, another task force member and President of the Foreign Policy Association, offered the "middle manpower" doctrine to justify this plan. In a report he argued that underdeveloped nations had much unskilled labor and adequate top leadership, but faced a critical shortage of personnel with college or technical training in teaching, crafts, farming, and organizational skills; correcting this "middle-level deficiency" became a primary Peace Corps objective. Senator Humphrey, Representative Reuss, Gordon Boyce, Director of the Experiment in International Living, and Warren Wiggins, Deputy Director of the United States foreign aid program constituted the remainder of the task force.

Before completing a report to the White House in late February, Shriver also received the report of the Colorado Research Foundation. Study director Maurice Albertson suggested areas where volunteers could be most useful (education, community development, health, and sanitation), stated conditions for Peace Corps service, and reported on visits to projects in Asia, Africa, and Latin America, which could use up to five thousand volunteers. Albertson was enthusiastic about prospects for a United States Peace Corps, pointing to the success of two hundred British youths working in underdeveloped countries through Britain's Voluntary Service Organization.

On March 1, 1961, President Kennedy established the Peace Corps by executive order on a "temporary pilot basis." Theodore Sorenson, Kennedy's special assistant, wrote the executive order from a draft by Edwin Bayley, who had been hired to be the Peace Corps' Director of Public Information. Bayley recalls:

The moment I showed up [in late February], they gave me a desk, a typewriter and several documents and told me to write the executive order declaring the formation of the Peace Corps. "What's it going to do?" I asked, foolishly. "That's for you to figure out from those papers," they said. The documents were the Reuss bill, the Humphrey bill, a transcript of Kennedy's remarks at Michigan—just a sentence or two—

46. Sullivan, *Peace Corps*, pp. 30–31.

the Albertson study [and] an ICA study by a team headed by Warren Wiggins.[47]

Funds from the Mutual Security Act would be used to have several hundred volunteers trained and working before the end of 1961. In using an executive order to create the Corps, Kennedy had to balance the gains in proving that such a plan was feasible against the losses involved in threatening congressional prerogatives.

The action did evoke substantial criticism, ranging from the age of members ("Kennedy's Kiddie Korps") to the title of the organization, "peace" being a propaganda term held to be the exclusive property of the Communists. The title was retained partly because that was the way it had been introduced and partly as a concession to Senator Humphrey, who argued that the word should be rehabilitated.[48] The only element of criticism at this point that led to later change was aimed at the Peace Corps' intention to contract with American religious organizations for special overseas projects; the church-state controversy invited by this and by the antiproselytizing agreement that such organizations would have had to sign led to the abandonment of the idea.

In the six months while the Peace Corps existed through executive order, Director Shriver and his highly collegial planning group (including Bayley, Wiggins, Morris Abram, Gordon Boyce, Harris Wofford, and a few others) set three policies that were to continue unchanged after congressional "creation" of the agency. First, volunteers were to be "doers" rather than advisers, working at the grassroots level rather than at the usual Agency for International Development (AID) level as some had suggested. Second, Peace Corps volunteers would go only where they were formally requested (which of course meant that requests would have to be solicited). Third, recruitment, training, and overseas programming would be done by the agency, not contracted out.

On May 29, the President sent a draft bill to Congress making the Peace Corps a permanent agency and allocating $40 million to it for fiscal 1962. By the time the bills were introduced—by Humphrey in the Senate and by House Foreign Affairs Committee chairman

47. Personal communication, May 25, 1982.
48. Sullivan, *Peace Corps*, p. 34.

Thomas E. Morgan in the House—Shriver had already announced agreements to establish projects in Tanganyika, the Philippines, and Colombia.

The bill was endorsed in Senate hearings by those private groups that were engaged in similar efforts (e.g., Operation Crossroads Africa) and by long-time champions of a governmental program (e.g., Heinz Rollman). With only technical amendments, the bill passed the Senate Foreign Relations Committee 14 to 0 and the entire Senate by voice vote. The equivalent House hearings turned up similar endorsements in the House Foreign Affairs Committee, which reported the bill out unanimously. Floor action in the House added a loyalty oath, which conferees upheld. The conference report was accepted by both houses on September 21, 1961, and was signed into law by President Kennedy the next day.

The civilian control of atomic energy case illustrates inadvertent presidential participation in policy initiation; the Peace Corps case comes close to the exact opposite. Here there is no pressing need, no emergency, nothing that compels action except the fact that, willy-nilly, an idea somehow becomes attached to the entourage of a traveling presidential candidate in search of something to offer. Thus the Peace Corps case suggests the utility of considering separately two processes: one process invents an alternative, nurtures it, floats it into the subculture of decision-makers; another process searches for ideas, finds them, renovates them for immediate use, and exploits them politically. Policy initiation varies with respect to the separation in time and space of these two processes of invention and search. In the Peace Corps example, the two were easily identifiable as separate entities, with invention clearly preceding search; in the case of the Truman Doctrine, the search for an alternative precedes and is intertwined with the invention of the alternative ultimately chosen.

IV

Domestic Innovation

Our first case of innovation in domestic policy seems to follow the pattern suggested by the Peace Corps example rather than that suggested by the Truman Doctrine or civilian control of atomic energy. Useful distinctions among these cases reside in the acuteness of the perceived need, the immediacy of the external threat, and perhaps also the freshness of the problem, since old problems are likely to be defined in quite different ways by interest groups variously situated with respect to them.[1] Thus we may speculate that the existence of a crisis that produces agreement on what the problems are, such as existed among American officials after the dropping of the atom bomb and after the British decided to withdraw from Greece, greatly increases the probability of innovation and decreases the probability of inaction. To the extent that a common definition of a "need" can be created among decision-makers, innovation is possible. As we shall see, however, the mobilization of these common definitions can in other circumstances be an arduous process, entailing creativity and statecraft of a very high order.

1. THE COUNCIL OF ECONOMIC ADVISERS

On February 20, 1946, President Truman signed the Employment Act into law. Section four of that act provided for the creation in the Executive Office of the President of a Council of Economic Advisers (CEA), composed of three "exceptionally qualified" persons to be

1. This in fact seems to be what Wildavsky means by an "issue-context." See Aaron Wildavsky, "The Analysis of Issue-Contexts in the Study of Decision-Making," *Journal of Politics* 24 (November 1962): 717–732.

appointed by the President with the consent of the Senate.[2] The
purpose of the new Council was to be to

> analyze and interpret economic developments, to appraise programs
> and activities of the government . . . and to formulate and recommend
> national economic policy to promote employment, production, and
> purchasing power under free competitive enterprise.[3]

The first and primary duty of the Council was to "assist and advise the
President in the preparation of the Economic Report" to the Congress and the nation.[4]

The origin of the idea for this structural innovation has been traced
by Edwin Nourse, first chairman of the Council, to Lewis L. Lorwin,
his colleague during the 1930s at the Brookings Graduate School of
Economics and Government in Washington. Lorwin had stimulated
interest in the whole subject of economic planning in his Brookings
pamphlet, *Advisory Economic Councils*,[5] published in 1931.[6] Lorwin's pamphlet described some of the economic councils then in
existence in Europe. Those councils varied in a number of ways: in
methods of selection (some were chosen by governments, others by
trade associations); in interests represented (some were broadly representative of all economic interests, others more restricted); and in
function (some were part of the administrative apparatus of planned
economies and were given specific powers to regulate and direct
industry, while others were primarily vehicles for representing the
country's different economic groups in matters of social and economic
planning). The size of the councils varied, and some were composed
at least in part of government personnel who gave advice on technical
and policy matters.

For Lorwin, the need for and utility of an American counterpart to
the various European councils was obvious. In his view, a national

---

2. The principal source for this case is the prize-winning book by the late Stephen
K. Bailey, *Congress Makes a Law* (New York: Vintage Books, 1964).

3. Ibid., p. 229.

4. Ibid.

5. Washington, D.C.: Brookings Institution, 1931.

6. Edwin Nourse, *Economics in the Public Service* (New York: Harcourt, Brace,
1953), p. 44.

economic council designed to provide the country with a continuous picture of the "way economic life was going" might have attenuated the 1929 crash and averted the economic "floundering" that followed. Writing in 1931, Lorwin proposed that such a council be created, with 150 to 175 members representing different industries, recognized trade associations, labor unions, and consumer organizations. While the full council would meet but once a year, continuing work would be carried on by special committees.[7]

Soon after Lorwin's idea reached print, Senator Robert M. La-Follette, Jr., of Wisconsin, introduced a bill in the Senate establishing a National Economic Council to gather economic information, locate and bring attention to economic problems, and propose solutions. The Council would make an annual report to the President, with recommendations, if any, for legislation. The proposed Council was to be composed of nine members appointed by the President and confirmed by the Senate. The bill called for the inclusion of at least one expert in each of the following areas: industry, finance, transportation, labor relations, agriculture, and scientific management.[8]

Senator LaFollette was chairman of the Senate Committee on Manufactures, to which his bill was sent. In October of 1931, a subcommittee of which he was also chairman held hearings on his legislation. These lasted several weeks and included testimony from both proponents and opponents of the idea of long-range economic planning. After the completion of the subcommittee hearings, La-Follette introduced a revised version of his bill.

During this period, the severity of the Great Depression and the apparent failure of traditional approaches to the problem had increased general interest in economic planning. Although President Hoover showed little sympathy for such ideas,[9] numerous plans for prosperity had been submitted by various groups and individuals to

7. "Council to Advise Business Is Urged," *New York Times*, January 25, 1931.
8. Nourse, *Public Service*, pp. 44–45.
9. Herbert Stein argues, however, that Hoover was much more interested in issues of planning and economic data gathering than is generally believed. See *The Fiscal Revolution in America* (Chicago: University of Chicago Press, 1969), pp. 6–38. This is indicated also by President Hoover's appointment of the President's Research Committee on Social Trends, which published *Recent Social Trends in the United*

the Department of Commerce, which, in April 1932, published a list of over twenty-five persons and organizations sponsoring proposals for long-range economic planning. Several of these proposals received wide circulation. The United States Chamber of Commerce had, in 1931, proposed creation of a National Economic Council of three to five members. The Council under this plan would have been appointed by a nominating committee of the Chamber of Commerce. It would have been organized around representatives of the various industrial, agricultural, and labor groups throughout the country and would have functioned as a body of experts charged with examining the economic climate and making suggestions for needed legislation to Congress.

Another proposal that received widespread attention was the "Swope Plan," named after its proponent, Gerard Swope, President of the General Electric Company. In testimony before LaFollette's subcommittee, Swope recommended that all industrial and commercial companies with over fifty employees in each industry be encouraged to form a trade association under the supervision of a federal agency. Each industry's trade association would have a general board of administration with three representatives each from the public, the employer, and the workers. The associations would function to provide information to Congress and the business community in general on matters of inventories, volume of business, product standardization, and stabilization of prices.

Throughout 1932, LaFollette's committee continued to examine such ideas as these and generally to air the idea of a national economic planning policy. Minor efforts were also made in the House to introduce legislation embodying LaFollette's and others' recommendations. Although the Ways and Means Committee held hearings, no action was taken one way or another. It was, after all, an election year. With Roosevelt's election, interest in an economic council subsided in Congress in the face of the various proposals designed to meet

States, with a foreword by Herbert Hoover (New York: McGraw-Hill, 1933). See also the essay by Ellis W. Hawley in J. Joseph Huthmacher and Warren I. Susman, eds., Herbert Hoover and the Crisis of American Capitalism (Cambridge, Mass.: Schenkman, 1973), pp. 3–33.

specific needs that flooded its agenda.[10] Concern with a formal apparatus to deal with long-term problems declined as the New Deal focused attention on the immediate and visible disasters of the depression. Although an apparatus for national economic planning was not instituted directly by the government, the idea was kept alive by two private groups. In 1934 the National Economic and Social Planning Organization (later the National Planning Association) was founded by Lorwin and other experts and academics sharing his views. Through the ensuing years this organization examined a variety of economic problems and published reports on diverse subjects, such as national fiscal policy, labor-management relations, settlement of war contracts, and farm programs. In 1945 the Association published a paper entitled *National Budgets for Full Employment*[11] which, according to Nourse, "unquestionably sparked a great deal of the thinking that led up to the passage of the Employment Act of 1946."[12]

The second such group was the Committee for Economic Development (CED), an independent organization of liberal and moderate businessmen that in the mid-1940s grew out of the Business Advisory Council established in 1933 by Roosevelt's Secretary of Commerce Daniel Roper and out of some initiatives taken by businessmen associated with the University of Chicago, including William Benton and Paul Hoffman.[13] The CED's immediate concern was planning for peacetime utilization of facilities that had been designed for or converted to wartime production, and planning for the reemployment of returning military personnel. The CED had originally initiated a field program in conjunction with local Chambers of Commerce, but as reconversion developed smoothly (contrary to most predictions), restricted itself to research into broad areas of government and

10. See Pendleton Herring, *Presidential Leadership* (New York: Rinehart, 1940), pp. 52ff., for a compact account of legislative activity during the so-called hundred days of the early Roosevelt administration.

11. National Planning Association, *National Budgets for Full Employment* (Washington, D.C., Government Printing Office, 1945).

12. Nourse, *Public Service*, p. 60.

13. For details, see Robert M. Collins, *The Business Response to Keynes, 1929–1964* (New York: Columbia University Press, 1981), pp. 56–62, 81–87.

business policy. Both of these organizations performed research and advisory functions that had been sought by Senator LaFollette and others during the early 1930s.

But despite the failure of Congress to create a national economic council, planning per se was not left wholly to private efforts during this period. As early as July of 1933, President Roosevelt had created the National Planning Board under the PWA to help develop a comprehensive program of public works. The following year, by executive order, the body became the National Resources Board and was given a larger and more independent status. In the 1939 reorganization of the Executive Office, the body underwent an additional name change, becoming the National Resources Planning Board. As it was constituted, the NRPB had only a limited mandate to "collect, prepare, and make available to the President such recommendations, plans, data, and information as may be helpful to the planned development and use of national resources." By interpreting "national resources" broadly, however, the NRPB conducted studies in such apparently unrelated areas as population trends, the structure of the national economy, and consumers' incomes and expenditures. During the war years the Board increasingly came to refer to itself in its publications as the "planning arm of the executive office."[14]

In fact, however, the NRPB was an "arm" with little connecting tissue to the rest of government. Nourse states the generally accepted view that the Planning Board was "notably unsuccessful in making itself effective as an advisory agency in national policymaking."[15] There was no coordination and often no relationship between the Board's recommendations and the program of the President. Further, until late in 1941, the Board rarely even committed itself to the findings that it published; rather, such reports were usually undertaken by committees of technical experts or even single individuals. When the Board finally did begin to express collective attitudes on various economic issues, its position was strongly interventionist in its assumptions. The final work of the Board, for example, a 400,000-word report, *Security, Work, and Relief Policies*, spelled out the need for the government to take on the responsibility

14. Nourse, *Public Service*, p. 63.
15. Ibid.

for full employment and argued for the use of federal spending as a prime tool for maintaining economic stability.[16]

Stephen K. Bailey, in his well-known case study, argues that this report was "a powerful impetus to those forces which two years later combined to make possible the introduction of the Full Employment bill."[17] Unfortunately for the NRPB, the report also enraged those congressmen who opposed governmental intervention in the economy as barely concealed socialism. For many members of Congress, the idea of planning itself had totalitarian implications. Bailey writes, "For its prophetic ideas, the NRPB was killed by Congressional action in an appropriations bill three months after its . . . report had been issued."[18]

The unhappy experience of the NRPB seems to indicate that the need to institutionalize and centralize long-range economic planning was not widely recognized by Congress and was not among the President's priorities as late as 1943. Yet it was less than three years later that the Council of Economic Advisers was written into law. This change in attitude was a response both to the pressure of events and to the transformation of the idea of planning in the minds of the various political actors.

The events that transformed the desires of a few academics into a widely, almost universally, recognized political need are these. The wartime boom had produced domestic prosperity. The nation, and certainly the nation's political leaders, did not wish the postwar world to repeat the disastrous 1930s. Unfortunately, as Corinne Silverman has noted, most experts agreed that such an unhappy scenario was in the offing:

> As the Second World War drew to a close, many economists of all types . . . issued predictions of a postwar depression. The general tenor of their analysis, which was accepted in the main by government officials, was that the layoffs from defense plants, disappearance of overtime wages, and the unemployment of returning veterans, would result in a sharp fall in personal incomes. This in turn would restrict consumer purchasing power and result in a business spiral into depres-

16. W. H. Lawrence, "Post-War Program: Sweeping Proposal for Economic Cushions is Drafted by NRPB," *New York Times*, March 11, 1943.
17. Bailey, *Congress*, p. 27.
18. Ibid.

sion. Predictions of unemployment ranged from 8,000,000 to the Federal Reserve Bulletin's 20,000,000.[19]

These predictions ultimately proved incorrect, but they were believed at the time they were made, and this belief transformed the entire debate over economic planning. For although there were economists and congressmen who still adhered to the fatalistic view that depression was inevitable and had to be faced stoically, without action, this view was not widely shared among the nation's voters. As early as the fall of 1944, a *Fortune* poll showed that 68 percent of the people believed that the government should provide jobs in cases where private business could not do so.[20] Thus, although many experts felt that depression was inevitable, it was clearly not acceptable politically: this provided a context for the introduction and debate of the Full Employment bill.[21]

The second major change in attitude involved the nature of planning itself. As understood by most of the liberal economists of the day, planning involved blueprints for a government presence in the economy. In good times and bad, federal spending and taxation would be employed as a major tool for economic stability, as dictated by Keynesian economic theory. The science of economics would thus inform the government where and how it should act. At the time of the creation of the CEA, however, this view of planning was anathema to many congressmen and incomprehensible to others.[22] The final outcome of this basic disagreement was a compromise that gave the planners an important institutional role within the government, but restricted that role to recommendations ultimately subject to congressional approval.

19. Corinne Silverman, "The President's Economic Advisors," in E. A. Bock, ed., *Case Studies in American Government* (Englewood Cliffs, N.J.: Prentice-Hall, 1962), p. 302.

20. Bailey, *Congress*, p. 9.

21. Much the same process was going on at the same time in Great Britain, which resulted in the adoption of the Beveridge Report. See Geoffrey Smith and Nelson W. Polsby, *British Government and its Discontents* (New York: Basic Books, 1981), pp. 90–91. David Donnison gives a brief description of the background in "The Contribution of Research to Social Policies and Programmes" (London: Centre for Environmental Studies, February 1972, Mimeographed).

22. Bailey, *Congress*, pp. 13–36.

The fear of depression that led Congress to adopt the Employment Act also produced a desire for data that would warn of trouble in the economy. As Bailey says, one of the major objectives of the Act was to "place responsibility on the President for seeing to it that the economy was purposively analyzed at regular intervals, and that Congress was informed of economic trends and of the President's program to meet the challenge of those trends." This analysis was to fulfill the function of an "economic barometer," so that Congress would be aware of an impending depression and could take appropriate action.[23] Meteorological metaphors allowed participants for whom planning smacked of socialism to view the new apparatus in a more favorable light. Analogies that likened the economy to the weather provided reassurance that one was no more controllable than the other. Economists could be viewed as weather forecasters, not planners; disaster relief could be legitimately provided, if the disaster itself could not be staved off. In periods of relatively good "weather," the fact that there was still government intervention in the economy could be safely ignored.

The actual debates that preceded the creation of the CEA centered around these problems of (1) creating such a "storm warning" center and (2) creating obstacles to inhibit more comprehensive planning. The issue of the role and scope of planning surfaced initially in 1945 during the hearings of the Senate Banking and Currency Committee on a Full Employment bill submitted by Senator James E. Murray, a Montana Democrat.[24] As envisioned by Murray, the planning requirements were relatively simple and the policy alternatives circumscribed. The problem of estimating the expenditure requirements necessary to assure full employment would be left to the President "in consultation with the members of his Cabinet and other

23. Ibid., p. 13.
24. Murray's bill placed total responsibility on the President's office to assure full employment. The various administrative agencies would annually make a statistical estimate of the projected volume of private expenditures and the expenditures needed to maintain full employment. The government would then attempt to stimulate nongovernmental spending to eliminate any gap between estimates and projected needs. If these procedures proved insufficient, the government would itself increase investments and expenditures to amounts necessary to assure full employment. Bailey, *Congress*, pp. 37–60.

heads of departments and establishments."[25] The bill also provided that the President establish "such advisory boards or committees composed of representatives of industry, agriculture, labor, and state and local governments . . . as he may deem advisable for the purpose of advising and consulting on methods of achieving the objectives of this Act."[26]

In the Committee hearings, a minority of the senators feared that this provision left the locus of planning invisible and thus irresponsible. They pressed for an Office of the Director of the National Budget, arguing that planning of such a program would be "extremely complicated and cannot possibly be done by the President himself." Rather, they asserted, "It should be done by an identifiable group, responsible to the Congress and the people as well as to the President, and not by an anonymous group of economic planners."[27] The liberal sponsors of the Senate bill were successful in rejecting any "specific administrative framework" that might have impaired the President's freedom of action.[28]

In the House, however, the unfriendly Committee on Expenditures in the Executive Department rejected Murray's entire bill by a 17 to 3 vote and appointed a special five-man subcommittee to draft a new bill. The swing member of this committee was Representative Will Whittington of Mississippi, who was soon given the major responsibility by his colleagues for drafting the substitute legislation. Whittington desired to get away from definite government commitments for expenditures, while still providing a framework of future crisis planning. This view was supported during the full Committee hearings by Dr. George Terborgh of the Machinery and Allied Products Institute. Whittington was impressed by Terborgh's testimony, and the subcommittee consequently asked him to draft a bill embodying his views. In addition to arguing against the view of government spending as a "panacea" for all economic ills, Terborgh warned of the danger of "hidden" planners within the government. "Both the economic analysis and the economic policy," he noted,

25. Ibid., p. 51.
26. Ibid., p. 168.
27. Ibid.
28. *Senate Report* 583, pt. 2, 79th Cong., 1st sess., September 24, 1945, 36.

may be prepared and promoted by men unknown to the public, whose appointment has not been confirmed by Congress, and who have no formal public responsibility. . . . This set-up invites behind the scenes manipulation by Presidential advisors of the moment, possessed, it may be, both by a passion for anonymity and a passion for controlling national economic policy . . . the arrangement is bad . . . the Federal Government . . . ought to make better organizational provision than is made in this bill.[29]

To offset this danger Terborgh proposed a

small independent commission . . . appointed by the President and confirmed by the Senate, whose responsibility it should be to make continuous study of the art of business stabilization through federal action. . . . The commission should be required to issue periodic reports to the President, the Congress, and the public, giving both its findings and its recommendations for federal policy, accompanied by a full statement of dissenting views.[30]

This proposal interested Representative Whittington, who saw in it several useful safeguards. Late in November he sent a draft bill providing for a council of economic advisers to Secretary of the Treasury Fred Vinson for comments. This draft provided for the Council to be a completely independent agency in the executive branch, with members appointed by the President for fixed five-year terms and subject to confirmation by the Senate. All reports of the Council to the President would be made available to a joint congressional committee for review. Vinson's argument that a fixed term of office would provide situations where a newly elected President might have an economic report drafted by men not of his own choosing persuaded Whittington to drop this provision. The provision making all reports public, which sponsors of the original bill contended was designed to embarrass the President when his proposals disagreed with Council recommendations, was retained over Vinson's objections by Whittington, but was finally dropped in the conference report.

With these changes, Whittington's proposal became the final provision in the Employment Act creating the CEA. By making the

29. Bailey, *Congress*, p. 169.
30. Nourse, *Public Service*, p. 73.

members of the Council visible and responsible to Congress (because they would be subject to confirmation), the antiplanning senators would have the opportunity to fight ideologically unacceptable nominees.

Though the institution was created in 1946, the ability of the Council to fulfill the tasks of economic planning envisioned for it by some economists was not to surface immediately. Later, in the early 1960s under Walter Heller's chairmanship, the Council did prove to be an effective instrument for the orientation of fiscal policy along explicitly Keynesian lines.

The recession of 1957–58, which might have appeared both inevitable and acceptable if it had occurred in 1946, became a major political issue in 1960. Keynesian notions had become both more widely disseminated during the 1950s among congressmen and businessmen and more legitimate, as government intervention in the economy failed to produce the disasters predicted by conservatives. As the climate of opinion changed and the economy came to be viewed less as an uncontrollable force, the idea that the government had a responsibility to provide for continuing prosperity rather than simply to accept the burden of acting to alleviate periods of sharp adversity grew in political strength. Nourished by this climate, and by a President who could be persuaded to accept the recommendations of theorists, the CEA under Walter Heller in the Kennedy administration abandoned purely barometric functions in favor of comprehensive recommendations for government action in a period of relative economic stability. The 1962 tax cut, the most immediate and visible demonstration of this new role, was not only accepted but applauded in Congress. Thus sixteen years after the camel's nose first entered the tent, the rest of the camel finally came inside.[31]

In talking about the "creation" of the Council of Economic Advisers, then, it is necessary to distinguish three processes: an invention process, in which ideas for something like an economic council floated around in Washington and in semiacademic circles; a search process, culminating in the moment when Representative Will Whit-

31. See Walter Heller, *New Dimensions in Political Economy* (Cambridge: Harvard University Press, 1966); Herbert Stein, *Fiscal Revolution*, pp. 281–454; Norman Macrae, "The Neurotic Trillionaire," *Economist* (May 15, 1969): 26–35.

tington, impressed by some testimony at a hearing, caused a provision for a council to be slipped into the draft of a bill that eventually became law; and an elaboration process, beginning with an administrative shell that in due course became a powerful agency.

Thus it is nearly impossible to say, except arbitrarily, when the Council of Economic Advisers "really" began. The agency came out of an ascertainable background, had a discernible beginning in a formal sense, but grew to its full stature much later on. The paternity of the agency is thus in some sense shared by Lewis Lorwin, George Terborgh, and Walter Heller—and perhaps by one or more of Heller's predecessors, such as the extremely effective Arthur Burns.

It is useful to contemplate this sort of piecemeal, drawn-out policy initiation, since it contributes a reminder that remodeling may be as effective a method of innovation as building an institution from scratch. The amount of recycling we have seen—in which proposals are made, defeated, and reemerge later on—in the test ban treaty, in the creation of the Atomic Energy Commission, and in the establishment of the Council of Economic Advisers, suggests that at any point in history there is a limited stock of ideas that provide an agenda for policymakers. Keeping these ideas afloat is an activity in which political leaders interact with the specialists who invent the ideas in the first place. Over time, these ideas are frequently modified as they are adapted for political use. The fears of conservatives that such proposals as those in which the early Council of Economic Advisers was embedded would lead to strong governmental intervention in the economy were, of course, eventually justified. But by then the political climate had changed so much that objections on doctrinal grounds carried little weight.

2. NATIONAL HEALTH INSURANCE FOR THE AGED

The adoption of the Medicare program is an example of a "chronic" issue in which a consensus about the nature of the problem and what to do about it is slow to form. There was a period of over eighty years between the first adoption by a foreign government of a health insurance program and the final success in the United States in 1965 of something similar, and a period of over fifty years between the drafting of the first American bill on the subject and the ultimate passage of one of its direct descendants. In this lengthy time period, the idea overcame opposition in both houses of Congress and in the presidency and passed through the period before 1930 when such governmental innovations in America were expected to be dealt with on a state-by-state basis.

During this extended period, the idea of national health insurance took on sharp partisan overtones. Many of the differences between the major parties on domestic matters that continue down to the present were formed in the 1930s, when government health insurance received its first presidential mention. These differences were clearly engaged when President Truman made national health insurance a part of his program after the Second World War. While Truman was able to propel the issue into national prominence, he lacked the votes in Congress to legislate. For the following eight years, the Republican party had control of the presidency and did not support government-funded health insurance. It was not until after the Democratic electoral landslide of 1964 that this "need," which had been a source of domestic agitation for fifty years, was in some sense met by an effective congressional enactment.

It is probably impossible to say definitively when the idea of national health insurance was first broached in intellectual and political circles by interest-group representatives, academics, or governmental officials. The German Reichstag under the leadership of Chancellor Bismarck was, at any rate, the first government to initiate such a program. The 1883 German plan was a compulsory sickness insurance law for limited groups of industrial laborers, later extended to certain classes of agricultural and white-collar workers. By the time of the passage of the British plan in 1911, eleven other European nations had enacted some form of government health insurance.[32]

In 1911, state-enacted workmen's compensation laws first withstood the test of the courts in the United States. European health statutes had attracted the attention of reform-minded Americans from the beginning, but interest in them did not spread much beyond

---

32. Forrest A. Walker, "Compulsory Health Insurance: The Next Great Step in Social Legislation," *Journal of American History* 56 (September 1969): 290–304. See also Peter Flora and Arnold J. Heidenheimer, eds., *The Development of Welfare States in Europe and America* (New Brunswick, N.J.: Transaction Books, 1981), pp. 17–183.

academic and social welfare groups (e.g., the National Conference of Charities and Correction), and workmen's compensation was as close to social insurance as the United States would come until the mid-1930s.

The most active group in agitating for a national health insurance system was the American Association for Labor Legislation (AALL), formed in 1907; in 1915, the AALL's Committee on Social Legislation presented the Association with its "Standard Bill," the first specific proposal of its kind in America and the focus of argument until the mid-1940s. In 1916, the American Medical Association (AMA) formed its Committee on Social Insurance, at the instigation of AMA member Dr. Alexander Lambert, who had also been on the drafting committee of the AALL and was former president Theodore Roosevelt's personal physician; the AMA at this time was a leading Progressive Era reform group, which chided the government on its weak public health laws. The AMA committee endorsed the Standard Bill.

Fifteen state legislatures considered the bill in 1917, but only in New York did it escape from committee, and even there it was able to pass only one house. The attention of the national government was focused on foreign affairs and on the imminent involvement of the United States in the First World War. This was one main reason why the Standard Bill met with so little success; another was the nature of the opposition. The most militant and organized of the Standard Bill's opponents were insurance companies. They were joined by business groups in general, who argued that a voluntary private system was what was needed. By 1920 they were also joined by the medical profession, in what was called a "United Front"; the 1920 AMA convention condemned any compulsory health insurance regulated by state or federal government. Finally, there was organized labor. Although the AALL had developed the Standard Bill, the American Federation of Labor condemned it in 1916 as "governmental interference." The AFL argument was that any economic activity attached to the police powers of the state was likely to be inimical to the welfare of the workers, a position which it took as long as Samuel Gompers was its leader.

> The leadership [of the AALL] published convincing studies of the need for a comprehensive health program, developed a plan of action in the Standard Bill, and launched a vigorous campaign to get it adopted

by the states. But the public did not respond. Somehow, interest never penetrated to the level of the workingman. It remained an intellectuals' movement. Without popular backing, the reformers could not overcome either the effects of preoccupation with the war or the well-organized campaign of the "United Front."[33]

The only national action on health matters in the 1920s was a 1922 law, viewed by the AMA as a step toward compulsory health insurance, that provided grants-in-aid to states for maternal and child care. The issue of a compulsory national health plan was raised again in 1934, when President Franklin D. Roosevelt's Committee on Economic Security considered it in relation to its planned Social Security bill.

> When in 1934 the Committee on Economic Security announced that it was studying health insurance it was at once subjected to misrepresentation and vilification. In the original social security bill there was only one line to the effect that the Social Security Board should study the problem and make a report to Congress. That little line was responsible for so many telegrams to members of Congress that the entire social security program seemed endangered until the Ways and Means Committee unanimously struck it out of the bill.[34]

The uproar apparently alerted President Roosevelt to the danger that a health program could pose to his Social Security plans, and he sent the Social Security bill to Congress with a message stating that he was "not at this time recommending the adoption of the so-called health insurance"; the success of the Social Security bill of 1935 apparently alerted the AMA to the possibility that this would be a "foot-in-the-door" for "socialized medicine," and it switched from opposing to actively supporting private health insurance alternatives. In that same year, Senator Arthur Capper of Kansas did introduce a bill to provide the medical care that had been struck out of the Social Security bill, but the bill never received committee hearings.

Although various governmental committees and national confer-

---

33. Walker, "Compulsory Health Insurance," pp. 303–304.

34. Statement by Edwin E. Witte, executive director of the Committee on Economic Security, cited in Theodore R. Marmor with Jan S. Marmor, *The Politics of Medicare* (Chicago: Aldine, 1970), p. 8. For the period 1932–1943, see Daniel S. Hirshfield, *The Lost Reform* (Cambridge: Harvard University Press, 1970).

ences discussed compulsory health insurance, the next bill in Congress to receive widespread public attention was that of Senator Robert Wagner of New York in 1939, but attention to it was cut off by the coming of the Second World War. In response to the Social Security Board's eighth annual report to Congress in 1943, which specifically called for a comprehensive national health insurance program to be incorporated into the Social Security Act, Wagner, Senator James Murray of Montana, and Representative John Dingell of Michigan (father of the contemporary congressman of the same name) introduced such a bill. The Wagner-Murray-Dingell bill covered preventive, diagnostic, and curative services by a physician of the family's choice, services of specialists, hospital care, laboratory and X-ray services, expensive medicines, and special appliances and eyeglasses; these would be available to all age groups. Every qualified doctor, dentist, nurse, and hospital would be eligible to participate, but none would be required to do so. Administration of the program would fall largely to the states, subject to federal standards; it would be financed through a payroll tax, with special services to come from general revenue. Introduction of the Wagner-Murray-Dingell bill became an annual event from 1943 through 1950, but the bill could not even obtain committee hearings before 1949 and never emerged from committee.

In 1945, three men who had all been connected with the 1934 Committee on Economic Security (the first national government unit to raise the health care issue)—Arthur Altmeyer, chairman of the Social Security Board, Wilbur Cohen, Altmeyer's technical adviser, and I. S. Falk, director of the Social Security Board's Bureau of Research and Statistics—made a deliberate effort to interest President Truman in the Wagner-Murray-Dingell proposal, an effort that was rewarded with a November presidential message to Congress calling for a comprehensive prepaid medical insurance plan for all Americans, to be financed through a 0.5 percent raise in the Social Security Old Age and Survivors' Insurance (OASI) tax. Congress took no action in 1946, however, and the Republican congressional majority was not in sympathy with this part of the President's program in 1947 and 1948. With a Democratic congressional majority returning in 1949, President Truman again called for health insurance for all ages, in both the State of the Union message and a special April

Health message; hearings were finally held on the Wagner-Murray-Dingell proposal, generating acrimonious debate but no action. The nominal 263-to-171 Democratic majority in the Eighty-first Congress could not be mobilized on government health insurance because of the probable defection of almost all southern Democrats.

Because Truman could not even gain congressional hearings on the matter in 1950, his Social Security advisers undertook a reevaluation of the administration's position in 1951, aimed at getting congressional agreement to a more limited program. Wilbur Cohen and I. S. Falk suggested limiting health care to those on Old Age and Survivors' Insurance, and, after clearing the proposal with Truman, Federal Security Agency Director Oscar Ewing called for amending the Social Security law to provide up to sixty days of hospitalization for those on Social Security, a service that could be provided without raising existing payroll taxes. This retreat from comprehensive coverage was to give the proposal a specific interest-group constituency, but also redefined the underlying need by drastically limiting the scope of the proposed program. As Theodore Marmor wrote:

> What had begun in the 1930s as a movement to redistribute medical services for the entire population turned into a proposal to help defray some of the hospital costs of social security pensioners. . . . In October of 1951 presidential assistant David Stowe outlined for Truman three ways of responding to the bleak legislative prospects for general health insurance: "softpedal the general health issue; push some peripheral programs in the area but not general insurance; or appoint a study commission to go over the whole problem." Three days later Truman accepted his staff's recommendation to create a study commission and charged them with finding "the right people" [as clients of the program].[35]

In April 1952, Senator Murray and Senator Hubert Humphrey, along with Representative Dingell, sponsored legislation to effectuate this recommendation, calling for insurance against the cost of sixty days of hospital care for aged persons covered by federal Old Age and Survivors' Insurance, their dependents, and survivors of deceased married persons. There was little congressional attention to

35. Marmor, *Politics of Medicare*, pp. 14–16.

it either in 1952 or upon its reintroduction in 1953; Dingell continued to introduce the bill until his death in late 1955, but got no action.

The Democratic platform of 1948 had emphasized medical care, but the 1950 defeat of several Democratic candidates who had campaigned for health insurance may explain why the 1952 Democratic platform did not mention it; the Republican candidate came out strongly against "socialized medicine." With newly elected President Eisenhower unsympathetic, backed by virtually all Republicans in Congress, and hostile Democrats overrepresented on key congressional committees, health care proposals initiated from 1952 to 1959 languished.

In 1956, however, a group of men who had been instrumental in creating the limited health care proposal of 1951 began to try to reactivate the issue by stimulating public and congressional interest. The most important among these were Cohen, then a professor at the University of Michigan; Falk, then a consultant for the United Mine Workers; Robert Ball, a career official with the Social Security Administration; and Nelson Cruikshank, head of the AFL-CIO's Social Security department. All were specialists in the field of social welfare.

Union contracts had already gained benefits for working members far above those of the Murray-Dingell bills of the late 1940s, and the AFL-CIO was eager to see those benefits continued after retirement. The result was a bill from the AFL-CIO Social Security division to provide 120 days of combined hospital and nursing home care, plus all hospital surgery; this would be paid through the Social Security system and financed by a 0.5 percent increase in payroll taxes (0.25 percent from employers, 0.25 percent from employees, and 0.375 percent from the self-employed). All OASI members and their surviving wives and dependents would be eligible, roughly 80 percent of those over sixty-five. The fourth-ranking Democrat on the House Ways and Means Committee, Aime J. Forand of Rhode Island, agreed reluctantly to introduce the bill, after the three more-senior members refused; he was to introduce it every year through 1960.

No presidential message or television appeal supported it; no crisis compelled attention to it; it had no status as a party measure in Congress; its sponsor was a little-known congressman who could not bring national attention to it and, indeed, did not try; its existence was not reported on the front pages of the newspapers until *after* it had become a national political issue. Yet many thousands of people managed to learn of the bill's existence and join the "crusade" for its enactment. Support for the Forand bill began as a genuine grass roots movement— surely the most phenomenal such movement of the period.[36]

The national movement for health care for the aged (principally hospital insurance) was one of the major national party issues of the early 1960s. Public interest in this movement was probably not importantly stimulated by the AFL-CIO campaign for the Forand bill or even by the AMA campaign against it (although Forand credited the AMA largely with calling it to the attention of the aged).[37] Rather, it was the 1959 hearings of Senator Patrick McNamara's Subcommittee on Aging. The Subcommittee was created by chairman Lister Hill of the Senate Labor and Public Welfare Committee. It held hearings in seven cities in 1959 on problems of the aged and aging, and a focus on health care emerged as a major concern. The response to these hearings led McNamara and eighteen fellow Democrats (including presidential hopefuls Hubert Humphrey, John F. Kennedy, and Stuart Symington) to introduce a revised version of the Forand bill by the end of 1959. The American Nurses Association broke with the AMA and endorsed the Forand bill's principle of funding through Social Security, and the American Hospital Association, while not ready for the same endorsement, asked the Eisenhower administration to study the problem. The House Ways and Means Committee took no action on the Forand bill, but it, too, asked for a study.

Unable to ignore these requests and the publicity generated by the McNamara hearings, HEW Secretary Arthur Flemming worked throughout 1959 to find a proposal that would satisfy interested parties within the administration and congressional Republicans. Flemming first suggested a plan under Social Security much like Forand's, but got no support for it from the administration. The "Medicare" plan (the first use of this name, and the only surviving feature of the Flemming proposal), which he announced in May

---

36. James L. Sundquist, *Politics and Policy: The Eisenhower, Kennedy, and Johnson Years* (Washington, D.C.: Brookings Institution, 1968), p. 297.

37. See Richard Harris, *A Sacred Trust* (New York: New American Library, 1966), on AMA lobbying.

1959, was a voluntary plan that would be available to all those with incomes below a certain level who paid a small annual premium. It covered the first $400 of family medical costs and would be financed jointly by the states and the federal government, with funds from the latter coming out of general revenue. Democrats attacked the plan for its income test, and for the administrative problems in getting all fifty states to pass enabling legislation and then appropriate their share of the money; Republicans were hardly less gentle, seeing the beginning of "socialized medicine," and the plan was never even introduced in the House.

> "This will be a small hole through which all will be driven, and the government will eventually be doing it all," [said] Senator Everett Dirksen of Illinois. . . . He was echoed by House Minority Leader Charles Halleck of Indiana. "If people were dying right and left for lack of medical care you'd read about it in the papers," said Halleck. Barring such news, he argued, the whole problem should be left to state and local governments.[38]

The Forand bill had the opposition of Senate Majority Leader Lyndon Johnson, Senate Finance Committee chairman Harry Byrd, House Speaker Sam Rayburn, and House Ways and Means Committee chairman Wilbur Mills, so it fared no better. A test vote in the Ways and Means Committee in March 1960 showed only eight of the twenty-five members for the Forand bill, but the approaching 1960 presidential campaign began to have an effect. Presidential hopeful Lyndon Johnson, later that year his party's vice-presidential candidate, changed his view and supported the bill, as did Speaker Rayburn, who asked Mills to reconsider it.

Mills was aware that a majority on his committee did not favor the Forand bill. He also knew that Arkansas would undoubtedly lose as many as two congressional seats after the 1960 census. This meant that within a couple of years he might face a more conservative opponent who might also be a sitting congressman and who could make Mills's support for the Forand bill a serious political liability.[39]

38. Sundquist, *Politics and Policy*, p. 303.

39. Mills's sense of caution no doubt was fortified by his memory of what had happened to the revered Brooks Hays, his colleague from Little Rock, who in 1958 had been beaten by a write-in candidate in the general election because of his conciliatory views on race relations. *Congressional Quarterly Almanac* (Washington, D.C.: Congressional Quarterly, Inc., 1958), p. 726.

Mills sponsored a plan that tracked with AMA testimony in opposition to the Forand bill, which followed the public welfare approach—direct assistance for the indigent aged only. The federal government would share with the states the cost of medical care for those over sixty-five whose incomes were determined by state standards to be inadequate; each state could join or not and could determine its program's content. No fees could be charged, and federal costs would come from general revenue. This amendment was added to a bill liberalizing Social Security benefits, and, under the usual closed rule for Ways and Means bills, it passed the House 381 to 23.

When the Senate reconvened after the national party conventions, Finance Committee member Senator Clinton Anderson (D-N.M.) introduced an amendment to the Social Security liberalization bill that embodied Democratic nominee Kennedy's approach. The Anderson amendment expanded the Forand bill's coverage to a maximum of 365 days of hospital care, 180 days of nursing home care, or 365 days of visiting nurse service per year; otherwise, all its provisions were more conservative. The retirement age was pushed back to sixty-eight, and younger dependents and survivors were cut out; the coverage of fees for surgery, physicians, or drugs outside of the hospital were removed; the first $75 of hospital care would be covered by the individual. Although this was the program of the Democratic party in 1960, only five of the eleven Democrats on the Senate Finance Committee supported it, and the Committee reported out the Mills plan, liberalized slightly by Senator Robert Kerr. The battle then moved to the Senate floor.

Senator Jacob Javits (R-N.Y.) offered a substitute, which followed the Flemming (Eisenhower administration) proposal closely except for elimination of the deductibility feature under which the first $400 of costs were covered by the family. It failed of adoption by a vote of 28 to 67, with no Democratic support. Then the Anderson bill, co-sponsored by presidential candidate Kennedy and vice-presidential candidate Johnson, failed by 44 to 51, with nineteen southern and border Democrats defecting to defeat it. The Kerr-Mills bill, which remained, passed and was signed into law by President Eisenhower.

Upon his election as President later in 1960, Kennedy asked Wilbur Cohen to head a task force to draft a Medicare bill. The draft closely resembled the Anderson bill of the previous year; it was introduced in the Senate in 1961 by Anderson, and in the House, where Ways and Means chairman Wilbur Mills was still opposed, by the next-senior member of the Committee, Representative Cecil King of California.

A massive propaganda campaign was waged by both proponents and opponents of the measure. At the close of the White House Conference on Aging in January 1961, 150 to 200 delegates formed an ad hoc committee to set up a permanent organization of senior citizens favoring King-Anderson; many of these delegates had been part of the "Senior Citizens for Kennedy" committees during the campaign, and the organization they set up, the National Council of Senior Citizens, was to have 525,000 members and 900,000 supporters under sixty-five by the end of 1961. The recently retired congressman Aime Forand was its chairman. The AMA countered with a campaign against "socialized medicine," featuring much national advertising and a letter-writing campaign to congressmen and spending from three to seven million dollars in the process.[40]

In the fall of 1961, Senator Pat McNamara took his Subcommittee on Problems of the Aged on the road again, holding hearings in thirty-one cities in thirteen states, listening to over two thousand witnesses, and gathering thousands of pages of testimony. Both the

---

40. Sundquist, *Politics and Policy*, p. 310. Richard Harris wrote:

The A.M.A. hierarchy and representatives from all the state medical societies held a special two-day meeting in Chicago a month after the King-Anderson bill was introduced. Conducted in strict secrecy—a squad of private policemen made sure that all outsiders stayed outside—the meeting was devoted largely to a discussion of the A.M.A.'s plans for its all-out effort. Various materials were passed around, including a thick "Do-It-Yourself Kit," which was later distributed in bulk to the Association's two thousand state and county medical societies. Among the items it contained were "fact sheets" that defended the Kerr-Mills program and attacked Medicare on statistical grounds; speeches for delivery to medical audiences; speeches for delivery to non-medical audiences; press releases announcing that the speeches had been delivered; one-minute radio advertisements; reprints of favorable editorials, articles, and public statements; sample letters-to-the-editor for local papers; advertising mats; leaflets, posters, and booklets; instructions to the women's auxiliary (doctors' wives) on how to conduct a letter-writing campaign that would produce three-quarters of a million letters to Congress by the end of the year; and descriptions of the best ways to line up support among influential organizations and citizens on the local level.

Harris, *A Sacred Trust*, pp. 126–127.

President and the AMA climaxed their efforts in May 1962, the President with a fighting "stump speech" before a large rally at Madison Square Garden, Dr. Edward Annis of the AMA with a speech to the near-empty Garden the following night.

As the debate wore on, congressmen reported that their mail shifted from favorable to unfavorable, and prospects for Ways and Means action, never good, disappeared. The only possibility for action was a compromise with Senator Javits and other Senate Republicans, which was tried next. The major difference between Senator Javits's bill and King-Anderson was Javits's proposal that the plan be administered through private nonprofit organizations and his insistence on three optional plans. With the choice between this and no bill, Kennedy agreed to go along. The compromise failed in the Senate anyway, by 48 to 52; thus, two years of intensive lobbying had produced a change in the Senate of one vote from the 1960 totals.[41]

Returns from the 1962 elections, bringing a net gain of three pro-Medicare Democrats to the Senate, removed that body as a roadblock for 1963, as long as the support of Senator Javits and his small bloc of pro-Medicare Republicans was available. In early 1963, Javits had set up his own national health care committee, composed of those favorable to federal action but opposed to parts of King-Anderson; this committee recommended hospital and nursing home care through Social Security and other medical services through private insurance plans, and Javits held out for these recommendations. King-Anderson supporters accepted them, and the King-Anderson-Javits bill passed as a rider on a bill liberalizing Social Security benefits in mid-1964, 49 to 44.

There was no hope for favorable Ways and Means Committee action, however, since that committee was still arrayed 13 to 12 against Medicare, with Mills and two other Democrats joining all ten Republicans in opposition. In conference, Mills and the two House Republican conferees, secure in the knowledge that Representative King had given up his attempt to have the House instruct its conferees to accept the Senate rider because he felt he could not get the

---

41. This includes the five unrecorded senators, allocated according to their announced or probable positions: hence the 1960 numbers would have been 47 to 53 if every senator had voted. Sundquist, *Politics and Policy*, p. 314.

votes, refused to accept the rider. Mills promised pro-Medicare Democrats on his committee, however, that Medicare would be the first priority for 1965 if they would back him in 1964. President Johnson countered by urging Senate conferees to hold out to the point of killing the entire Social Security liberalization bill, which they did, on the theory that it would be needed as a "sweetener" for Medicare the following year and that the payroll tax should not go to 10 percent before the establishment of Medicare.

The National Council of Senior Citizens calculated that the results of the election of 1964, a landslide against Barry Goldwater in the presidential race, meant at the congressional level an increase of forty-four House votes for Medicare. The bill, again introduced by Representative King and Senator Anderson, became H.R. 1 and S. 1 for 1965. The very large number of new Democrats in the House also meant a reorganization of the membership of the Ways and Means Committee, increasing the ratio of Democrats to Republicans and permitting the appointment of a pro-Medicare majority there for the first time ever.

The Committee began hearings in late January and was greeted with three separate proposals for some kind of health program. The first of these was the King-Anderson bill (née the Forand bill of 1956). It included a year of hospital care, nursing home care, or visiting nurse service, financed through the Social Security system for all those over sixty-five; it did not include surgery, physicians' fees, or drugs.

The AMA countered with its "eldercare" proposal, which was essentially an expansion of the Kerr-Mills Act to permit federal and state governments to purchase private health insurance policies for the needy aged; the means test was still present, but the fact that the proposal also covered doctors' fees meant that the AMA could claim that it was "more comprehensive" than the administration bill.

The ranking Republican on Ways and Means, John W. Byrnes of Wisconsin, would not introduce the AMA proposal (second-ranking Republican Thomas Curtis of Missouri did), but came out with his own "Byrnes bill" instead. To prevent the Democrats from getting all the credit for a bill that was clearly going to pass, Byrnes called for subsidies to enable elderly persons to buy private insurance policies. The program would be federal in both financing and administration;

the means test for participation was eliminated, but premium charges would be based on beneficiaries' incomes. Byrnes could rightly claim that his benefits were far broader than those of the King-Anderson bill, since they included drugs and doctors' and surgeons' fees.

Although most of the non-AMA criticism of King-Anderson before the Committee was aimed at that plan's limited benefits, HEW officials like Cohen who had experienced past defeats were reluctant to ask Congress for a broader program.

> The Byrnes and King-Anderson bills were presented as mutually exclusive alternatives. HEW officials were exhausted from weeks of questioning and redrafting, and viewed the discussion of the Byrnes bill as a time for restful listening. But Mills, instead of posing a choice between the two bills, unexpectedly suggested a combination which involved extracting Byrnes' benefit plan from his financing proposal. On March 2, Mills turned to HEW's Wilbur Cohen and calmly asked whether such a "combination" were possible. Cohen was "stunned," and initially suspicious that the suggestion was a plot to kill the entire Administration proposal. No mention had even been made of such innovations. Cohen had earlier argued for what he called a "three-layer cake" reform by Ways and Means: H.R. 1's hospital program first, private health insurance for physicians' coverage, and an expanded Kerr-Mills program "underneath" for the indigent among the aged. Mills' announcement that the committee appeared to have "gotten to the point where it is possible to come up with a medi-elder-Byrnes bill" posed a surprise possibility for a different kind of combination. That night, in a memorandum to the President, Cohen reflected on Mills' "ingenious plan," explaining that a proposal which put "together in one bill features of all three of the major" alternatives before the committee would make Medicare "unassailable politically from any serious Republican attack." Convinced now that Mills' strategy was not destructive, Cohen was delighted that the Republican charges of inadequacy had been used by Mills to prompt the expansion of H.R. 1.[42]

Following Byrnes, a supplementary voluntary program to subsidize surgery, physicians' fees, and drugs at a cost of $3 per month to the beneficiary and $500 million a year to government general revenue was added to the basic King-Anderson bill. The bill was reported

42. Marmor, *Politics of Medicare*, pp. 64–65. See also John F. Manley, *The Politics of Finance* (Boston: Little, Brown, 1970), pp. 118–121.

favorably on a straight party vote, 17 to 8. House debate was desultory; the motion to substitute the Byrnes plan failed by 191 to 236 (the margin of 7 to 58 among first-term Democrats making the difference), and the "eldercare" proposal of the AMA never even came to a vote. The measure that left the House was more liberal than the one the administration had sent in.

By changing from opponent to manager, Mills assured himself control of the content of H.R. 1 at a time when it could have been pushed through the Congress despite him. By encouraging innovation, and incorporating more generous benefits into the legislation, Mills undercut claims that his committee had produced an "inadequate" bill. . . . Mills' conception of himself as the active head of an autonomous, technically expert committee helps to explain his interest in shaping legislation he could no longer block, and his preoccupation with cautious financing of the social security system made him willing to combine benefit and financing arrangements that had been presented as mutually exclusive alternatives. The use of general revenues and beneficiary premiums in the financing of physicians' service insurance made certain the aged and the federal treasury, not the social security trust funds, would have to finance any benefit changes. In an interview during the summer of 1965, Mills explained that inclusion of medical insurance would "build a fence around the Medicare program" and forestall subsequent demands for liberalization that "might be a burden on the economy and the social security program."[43]

The Senate Finance Committee added some moderate liberalization of the House bill, and the bill passed the Senate 68 to 21. The conferees split the difference on most of the minor changes. A 307 to 116 House vote and a 70 to 24 Senate vote sent the bill to President Johnson, who signed it on July 30, 1965, at Harry Truman's Independence, Missouri, home.

The elapsed time from the first introduction of a health insurance bill in Congress in 1939 by Senator Robert Wagner to final passage of Medicare in 1965 was twenty-six years. By other measures, the matter of health insurance can be said to have been somewhere on the agenda of possible governmental action since the turn of the century. This is a history so venerable that it raises questions about

43. Marmor, *Politics of Medicare*, p. 69.

the relationship of what finally passed—federally funded medical insurance for the elderly—to its precursors, which were more comprehensive. Like the early proposals for the Council of Economic Advisers, early Medicare plans looked quite different from what finally emerged. In what sense, then, are the alternatives finally chosen "indebted" to earlier attempts? If earlier conceptions had not existed, how would the shape of alternatives finally chosen have changed?

Nobody knows the answer, but a few things can be said. A whole generation of technicians and experts—Wilbur Cohen is perhaps the foremost example—grew up in an atmosphere preoccupied with the failed agenda of the New Deal, including government-sponsored national health insurance. While improvisations at the last minute by Wilbur Mills clearly were crucial in determining how alternative policies were combined and which features ultimately were to survive to become law, the alternatives themselves could not have arrived at the House Ways and Means Committee if groups had not long before been mobilized to contest the merits of Medicare and to promote various alternative health insurance schemes.

This mobilization process was the work not of a few days, but of years. Of course there might have been a Medicare program enacted in 1965 if someone had had the wit to ask for it, even if Robert Wagner, James Murray, and John Dingell had not pressed for such a policy continuously two decades before. But we will never know by what alternative means this particular program, or one like it, might have worked its way into the permanent agenda of the Democratic party, and into the promises of Democratic Presidents and presidential candidates from Harry Truman forward.

This case suggests not that the long, hard road to policy initiation is one inevitably crowned with success, but only that there is such a road, and that some of the things that proponents of innovative policy alternatives do far back along that road—mobilizing support, doing technical research on the effects of various levels of government activity, trying out a variety of alternative means to the same or similar ends, and indoctrinating a generation of experts in the need for effort—may have an important effect on the outcome.

We can think of this process as policy incubation. Incubation is activity by the supporters of an innovation that occurs in the hiatus between the first appearance of an idea for a policy and its definitive entry into the enactment process. This process of incubation was particularly important for health insurance, since no such scheme met with immediate acceptance. Friends of this innovation had to bide their time, gather supporters, keep alert to the emerging salability of alternatives, and wait for a better day.

Like Will Whittington in the case of the Council of Economic Advisers, Wilbur Mills acted as a political broker, selecting among possible alternatives a politically viable combination. Neither was a long-time advocate of the measure he eventually brought to enactment; both took responsibility for channelling energies that were too strong for them to resist. Thus politically neutral—even mildly unfriendly—politicians can be enlisted to the cause of policy innovation when forces in the political system come together to demand that the search for a policy outcome bear fruit. Postwar worries about unemployment and the Goldwater landslide of 1964 provided two such occasions.

3. LOCAL PARTICIPATION IN COMMUNITY ACTION PROGRAMS

Title II of the Economic Opportunity Act of 1964 authorized the establishment of Community Action Programs (CAPs), a project designed to use the resources of an urban or rural area to reduce poverty or its causes "through developing employment opportunities, improving human performance, motivation, and productivity, or bettering the conditions under which people live, learn, and work." Each CAP was to be organized and developed by a nonprofit or private agency, and "conducted and administered with the maximum feasible participation of the residents of the areas and members of the groups served."[44]

The decision to use the community action idea to lead the attack on poverty was a result of two notions that found their way into the discussions of government decision-makers at approximately the same time. One was the idea that fiscal policy alone would not be sufficient to eradicate poverty and that more direct governmental

---

44. Peter Marris and Martin Rein, *Dilemmas of Social Reform* (New York: Atherton, 1967), p. 210.

action would be needed. The chief advocates of this theme were economists on the staff of President Kennedy's Council of Economic Advisers, who doubted they could reduce by other means the unemployment of persons socially situated in certain unreachable ways. Ideas about reaching the "structurally unemployed" had been extant among economists for some time.

The second notion was concerned with a method of direct action. Peter Marris and Martin Rein, in their authoritative book examining the development and problems of community action, assign to the Ford Foundation's "gray areas" projects credit for originating the community action approach.[45] These projects were an attempt to combat problems arising in the central city by methods other than physical redevelopment. The Ford Foundation's public affairs department saw a community school system as an essential resource in assisting the city's poor and especially poor minorities in gaining an opportunity for advancement. The schools—aside from their normal functions—could sponsor such projects as after-school activities for youth, work-study programs, adult education, counseling, and kindergartens. In 1960, these views (originally the brainchild of Henry Saltzman and Paul Ylvisaker, member and director respectively of the Ford Foundation's public affairs division) were translated into action through a series of grants to seven metropolitan school systems that allowed them to establish such programs. During the following year, three more systems were added to the list of grant recipients.[46]

From the beginning this purely educational strategy was viewed by Ylvisaker as only an initial phase of a larger, more comprehensive approach to the amelioration of community ills. He envisioned the ultimate effort as involving an attack on a wide range of related problems, to be launched through the integration of existing governmental and private efforts. There was, however, no single community agency with the authority to coordinate both public and private efforts in addressing a variety of problem areas. As a consequence, the Ford Foundation public affairs division concluded that new institutions would have to be created with broad enough authority to provide the necessary coordination. In December 1961, after

45. Ibid., pp. 7–32.
46. Ibid., pp. 16–17.

lengthy negotiations, the city of Oakland, California, was awarded $2 million for such a program. In 1962, grants for new corporations with varying powers were awarded in New Haven, Philadelphia, and Boston. In 1963, $7 million was awarded to North Carolina to stimulate programs throughout that state, and in 1964 the final of the six "gray area project" grants was awarded to a corporation in Washington, D.C.[47]

These new corporations were forerunners of the community action agencies. They gave to communities an organizational framework and money—in some cases, a considerable amount of money—to prescribe programs for their needs. Moreover, the corporations were intended to deal with many problems, using a variety of approaches.[48]

The gray area projects were not the first to suggest a community action agency. In 1957 the Board of Directors of New York's Henry Street Settlement on the Lower East Side initiated a "comprehensive" attack on the problems of their community. By 1958 the Settlement was convinced that the only way this project would obtain sufficient money would be to undertake it as research. They approached the Columbia University School of Social Work for assistance in developing a research design and obtained the assistance of two Columbia sociologists, Richard Cloward and Lloyd Ohlin. The Settlement, in conjunction with other community, civic, and social organizations, created a nonprofit membership corporation to develop and run the program. The organization was awarded a two-year planning grant by the National Institute of Mental Health (NIMH).[49]

Cloward and Ohlin, also consultants to the Ford Foundation, were just completing a book, *Delinquency and Opportunity*,[50] that would come to serve as the theoretical basis for the project, which was called Mobilization for Youth. They viewed juvenile delinquency as occurring when individuals are not allowed "socially prescribed" means of

47. Sundquist, *Politics and Policy*, p. 123.

48. See Russell D. Murphy, *Political Entrepreneurs and Urban Policy* (Lexington, Mass.: Heath Lexington Books, 1971), a thorough discussion of the New Haven experience.

49. Marris and Rein, *Social Reform*, pp. 5, 20, 44, 111, 119.

50. Richard Cloward and Lloyd Ohlin, *Delinquency and Opportunity: A Theory of Delinquent Gangs* (Glencoe, Ill.: Free Press of Glencoe, 1960).

accomplishing goals upon which the larger society has placed a value and which delinquent individuals have internalized. They became delinquent, according to this argument, only when denied an opportunity of achieving their goals through prescribed avenues. Thus, the conclusion was that the most effective way of ending delinquent behavior is to provide sufficient opportunity to achieve desired goals legitimately.

Until John F. Kennedy became President, these private endeavors had no visible impact on White House policy. Immediately after his inauguration, however, President Kennedy asked a close friend of his brother Robert and member of his campaign staff, David Hackett, to develop a new federal approach toward juvenile delinquency. Hackett, who had no special training or expertise in the area, was open to new ideas. Marris and Rein note the appeal that the gray areas project and Mobilization for Youth had for Hackett:

> He began to inform himself of current thinking, consulting with the National Institute [of Mental Health], the Children's Bureau, police officials, universities and research centres. At this time, when his ideas were still unformed, the Ford Foundation got in touch with him. David Hunter and Dyke Brown, who ran the Foundation youth programme, introduced him to the philosophy of Mobilization for Youth and the gray area projects, which set delinquency in the context of social frustration and alienation, and took the conventions of institutional practice as the principal target of reform. Innovative, intellectual, antibureaucratic, this line of thought appealed to the spirit of the new frontier, and Hackett was readily persuaded to align his own policy accordingly. He invited Lloyd Ohlin, as joint author of the theory which rationalized this policy of wide-ranging social intervention, and co-director of research at Mobilization, to help him develop the Federal programme. In the following months, while they revised legislation which had been put forward without success since 1955, they developed the idea of a special executive committee, with power to draw together the many Federal departments, institutes and bureaus concerned with delinquency.[51]

The strategic significance of expertise is once again apparent in this passage, as is the bifurcation between the two processes of invention of policy alternatives and of the search by political actors for politi-

---

51. Marris and Rein, *Social Reform*, p. 21.

cally feasible solutions, the Ford Foundation entering from one
direction, the Kennedy administration from the other.

Hackett's suggestion for an executive committee was acted on in
May 1961, when Kennedy created the President's Committee on
Juvenile Delinquency and Youth Crime, by executive order. The
Committee was to be composed of secretaries from three departments: Justice, HEW, and Labor. Each department assigned a special assistant: Hackett for the Attorney General, Ohlin for HEW,
and Pierre Salinger (the White House press secretary) for Labor. On
the same day as the executive order, President Kennedy sent Congress a message requesting funds to fight rising juvenile delinquency
rates. Congress responded in September by giving HEW and the
President's Committee $2 million for three years to spend on what
were then known as demonstration projects.

Hackett recruited a staff of individuals who had been involved with
similar efforts. Among them was Richard Boone, from the public
affairs department of the Ford Foundation, and William Lawrence,
who had worked with Ohlin in Mobilization for Youth.[52] During late
1961, both the Ford Foundation and the President's Committee staff
were surveying communities for possible programs. While they had
somewhat different views on how programs should be sponsored,
both organizations were addressing similar problems in similar ways.
Both were concerned not only with the development of comprehensive programs ranging from education to legal aid, but also with the
structure and composition of the governing agencies. They agreed on
the necessity of new structures to cut across old jurisdictional lines,
with representation to integrate the various existing programs and to
keep them geared to community needs. The grants from these two
bodies tended to go to the same communities. By the end of 1964
these joint efforts resulted in the creation of seventeen community
action agencies.[53]

One of the projects receiving grants from both the Ford Foundation and the federal government was Mobilization for Youth, which

---

52. Ibid., p. 23.

53. Ibid., p. 24. While there was no active collusion between the two groups (each
sent out independent teams to canvass and assess the various proposals), the similarity
of their goals led their grants to converge on the same cities.

had published a report entitled *A Proposal for the Prevention and Control of Delinquency by Expanding Opportunities*.[54] The report, which was a request for project funding from the NIMH, naturally based its approach on Ohlin's "opportunity theory." Daniel Patrick Moynihan comments in *Maximum Feasible Misunderstanding* on its contents:

> The volume is one of the more remarkable documents in the history of efforts to bring about "scientific" social change: lucid, informed, precise, scholarly, and above all, candid. A plan devised by a group of middle-class intellectuals to bring about changes in the behavior of a group of lower class youth who differed from them in ethnicity and religion, in social class and attitudes, in life styles, and above all, in life prospects. An enterprise, designed in the most avowed and open manner, to acquire by the experimental mode knowledge of general validity that could be applied elsewhere with predictable results.[55]

The Mobilization for Youth proposal called for many programs similar to those later found in the Economic Opportunity Act, such as preschool programs, youth job centers, neighborhood service centers, and so forth. Moynihan notes this similarity in approach:

> A striking quality about the MFY proposal is the degree to which its Program for Action corresponds in structure and detail to the Economic Opportunity Act that was presented to Congress two and a quarter years later, even, indeed, to the martial spirit of their popular designations, and the actual terminology in many instances. The community action title of the Economic Opportunity Act, for example, defines such a program as one that "mobilizes" public and private resources.[56]

The proposal received an enthusiastic response from its sponsors. Mobilization for Youth was awarded $12.5 million for three years through joint financing. The Ford Foundation contributed 15 percent; New York City, 30 percent; the NIMH, 36 percent; the Presi-

---

54. Mobilization For Youth, Inc., *A Proposal for the Prevention and Control of Delinquency by Expanding Opportunities* (New York: Mobilization for Youth, Inc., 1961).

55. Daniel Patrick Moynihan, *Maximum Feasible Misunderstanding: Community Action in the War on Poverty* (New York: Free Press, 1969), pp. 51–52.

56. Ibid., p. 56.

dent's Committee, 16 percent; and the Labor Department and other agencies, additional small amounts.[57]

Richard Blumenthal, in his account of the Kennedy administration's development of the antipoverty program, asserts that the idea of community action originally had little to do with the decision to declare a war on poverty. He states that the decisions to attack poverty and the methods of doing so were made "separately by different people, at different times, for somewhat different reasons."[58] The main proponents of the more basic theme—to attack poverty—were to be found in the Council of Economic Advisers. The decision to use the community action approach described above came later and was largely made within the Bureau of the Budget.

A leading proponent of community action at the Council was Robert Lampman, a Wisconsin economics professor on leave, who joined the CEA staff in 1962.[59] During the summer of 1963, Lampman circulated a paper arguing that proposed administration fiscal measures would do little to lessen poverty, a problem relevant to approximately a fifth of the nation's population. Lampman's analysis showed "a drastic slowdown in the rate at which the economy is taking people out of poverty.[60] He argued that instead of relying on such measures as a tax cut to give the poor jobs, direct action would have to be taken as well. Blumenthal describes the dilemma President Kennedy faced in deciding to attack poverty:

> Although Lampman continued his barrage of memoranda to the White House, President Kennedy's closest advisors were divided. None was really against the notion of fighting poverty, but many be-

57. Ibid., p. 58.

58. Richard Blumenthal, "The Bureaucracy: Anti-Poverty in the Community Action Program," in Allan P. Sindler, ed., *American Political Institutions and Public Policy* (Boston: Little, Brown, 1969), p. 142.

59. Lampman had already published extensively on the economic bases of social stratification. See, for example, Robert J. Lampman, *The Low Income Population and Economic Growth*, U.S. Congress Joint Economic Committee, Employment Growth and Price Levels, study paper no. 12 (Washington, D.C.: Government Printing Office, 1959); Lampman, *The Share of Top Wealth-holders in National Wealth, 1922–56* (Princeton, N.J.: Princeton University Press, 1962); and Lampman, ed., *Social Security Perspectives* (Madison, Wis.: University of Wisconsin Press, 1962).

60. Sundquist, *Politics and Policy*, p. 135.

lieved that it would lack political appeal and hence should be delayed until after the 1964 campaign. Theodore Sorensen, special counsel to the president, Charles Schultze, assistant director of the Budget Bureau, and Wilbur Cohen, assistant secretary of Health, Education and Welfare, warmly supported the program. But others, including Meyer Feldman, deputy special counsel to the president, and Willard Wirtz, secretary of Labor, were more cautious. President Kennedy himself worried about the timing of the measure. He was sensitive to warnings of a white backlash, and he acknowledged that the "middle class might feel threatened" if the government appeared to care only about the plight of the poor.[61]

During the 1960 presidential campaign, Kennedy had been moved by the problems of poverty he had seen in West Virginia. Also, he was known to have read Michael Harrington's book *The Other America*[62] and a very long article summarizing Harrington's argument by Dwight Macdonald in the *New Yorker*.[63] In June, Kennedy asked Council of Economic Advisers chairman Walter Heller to begin working on a legislative program. In October, Kennedy authorized development of a set of specific legislative recommendations for 1964. In mid-November, shortly before his assassination, he decided to make the antipoverty program a major legislative request and asked Heller to show him his proposals within the next two weeks.[64]

Assuming that the President would call for an antipoverty program for 1964, Heller and the CEA staff began planning as early as June. By November, Heller was convinced that any program should "concentrate on relatively few groups and areas where problems are most severe and solutions most feasible."[65] On November 5, he sent a memorandum to the various departments requesting that they submit suggestions on possible programs to the Budget Bureau.

One of the men in the Bureau of the Budget charged with developing concrete proposals was William Cannon, the assistant chief of the

61. Blumenthal, "The Bureaucracy," p. 144.

62. Michael Harrington, *The Other America* (New York: Macmillan, 1962).

63. Ibid., p. 144. Macdonald's article, entitled "Our Invisible Poor," appeared in the January 19, 1963, issue, pp. 82–132.

64. Harrington, *Other America*, p. 144; Sundquist, *Politics and Policy*, pp. 136–137.

65. Blumenthal, "The Bureaucracy," p. 145.

Bureau's Office of Legislative Reference.[66] Cannon, who had majored in political science at the University of Chicago and had later headed that school's development program, which, as he said, put him "up to my neck in the problems of the community," believed that new political institutions were needed to promote and direct social change. He was unimpressed by the departmental responses to Heller's memorandum. He then contacted David Hackett and asked him to present his views on how to approach the poverty problem.[67] Hackett recommended that the government set up task forces to study the problem for an entire year prior to making any major legislative recommendations. In the interim, a certain number of demonstration community action programs utilizing a comprehensive approach to poverty should be funded. Cannon found this proposal attractive in two respects: first, new structures would be created; and second, an initially limited number of projects would satisfy Heller and Assistant Budget Director Charles L. Schultze, who had argued that spending should be aimed at pockets of poverty.

In a mid-December joint CEA–Budget Bureau meeting, the officials "groped for the new idea that would distinguish and dramatize the anti-poverty program."[68] Cannon realized that development corporations were what they were looking for, and shortly thereafter, in a memorandum closely following Hackett's recommendations, he proposed that ten demonstration areas (five urban, five rural) be chosen and that a development corporation be created in each. These corporations would receive up to $10 million each for the creation of new plans and the coordination of existing programs attacking poverty.

Cannon's proposal received a favorable response from Schultze, who forwarded the proposal to Budget Director Kermit Gordon. Seeing that Gordon was hesitant, Paul Ylvisaker at the Ford Foundation called him, endorsing Cannon's plan. Meanwhile, administrators of several Ford Foundation–sponsored community corporations

66. On the role of the Bureau of the Budget in program development under the Kennedy administration, see Larry Berman, *The Office of Management and Budget and the Presidency, 1921–1979* (Princeton, N.J.: Princeton University Press, 1979), pp. 67–69.

67. Blumenthal, "The Bureaucracy," p. 147.

68. Sundquist, *Politics and Policy*, p. 138.

met with the Budget Bureau staff. The staff convinced Gordon, who responded by writing and circulating a memorandum entitled "An Attack on Poverty," which endorsed the community action idea. Gordon, with Heller's help, convinced President Johnson to accept the community action approach.[69]

President Johnson and his advisers were disappointed with the limited scope of Cannon's proposal. "What we said was, 'Go stage by stage, don't rush into the legislation,'" insists Hackett, "but Johnson just said, 'Go.' The word came down to move."[70] Blumenthal speculates that Johnson's desire to "move full speed ahead" may have been based on fears that the program would be labeled "tokenism."[71] Perhaps also Johnson himself felt a need to assert and establish a record of his own on this issue.[72] However, the timing placed him in something of a dilemma. Although he needed to display a large antipoverty program, he was currently in an economy drive, and he feared a major spending request would leave him vulnerable to conservative critics in Congress. He decided to take some of the single-purpose programs currently before Congress and tack them onto his poverty bill. Blumenthal explains the White House reasoning:

> This legerdemain would not only increase the apparent size of the program at no extra cost, but would also broaden its appeal. Particular interest groups with a direct stake in one of the single-purpose programs would throw their support behind the entire package.[73]

Thus community action agencies suddenly became an even more important segment of the government's total effort to relieve poverty.

The new idea of community organization was never fully grasped by President Johnson or his advisers. The Budget Bureau had left the impression that the agencies would be set up by the local governments. It would increase local executives' stake in the program, thus,

69. Ibid., p. 139.
70. Blumenthal, "The Bureaucracy." p. 151.
71. Ibid.
72. Ibid., pp. 150–151.
73. Ibid., p. 152.

it was hoped, garnering their support. Blumenthal notes Johnson's misunderstanding of the program, which the President saw as the chief avenue of the federal attack on poverty:

> The White House certainly never thought that the poor themselves would have any part in developing or administering the program. The president, according to his closest aides, apparently believed that . . . local governments . . . would operate the Community Action programs, rather than rely on separate corporations. Johnson continued in this misunderstanding until shortly after the legislation was passed.[74]

While the departments were less interested than the White House in the public appearance of the program, they too criticized Cannon's suggestion of limited demonstration programs. They also opposed making community action the only program to be included in the legislation. Several officials criticized the whole idea of community action. Assistant Secretary of Labor Moynihan argued that if CAPs were accepted, poor people would not get any of the money; rather, it would all go to middle-class planners. Secretary of Labor Wirtz argued that the money needed to be spent on job-training programs instead. HEW felt that sufficient apparatus existed to coordinate the various governmental efforts. The departments also raised jurisdictional questions that the community action idea created. Who would oversee the community agencies? Would the departments have control over the component programs of the community action agencies? Which, if any, single-purpose programs would be placed in the antipoverty package?

In response to White House and departmental objections, Gordon and the Budget Bureau had modified Cannon's draft. They grudgingly yielded on the size of the program and in a new draft raised the appropriation request for setting up these CAPs from $100 million to $500 million. From the beginning, however, the Budget Bureau saw the basic goal of community action agencies as coordinating existing institutions and programs in the legislation.[75] They suggested that an additional $500 million already budgeted for other programs be reserved for CAPs—but without including the programs themselves

74. Ibid., p. 153.

75. Daniel Patrick Moynihan, "What Is Community Action?," *Public Interest* 3 (Fall 1966): 5.

with the antipoverty package.[76] In the new draft the Budget Bureau avoided the questions of organization and jurisdiction at both the community and the federal levels. This new draft again kindled controversy among the departments. President Johnson, fearing that departmental infighting might kill the program, recruited Peace Corps director Sargent Shriver to head a task force to examine and make recommendations on the scope and structure of the antipoverty effort. Shriver's high prestige within the administration and with Congress, Johnson felt, might serve to reduce the criticism within the various departments. The staff of the task force was borrowed from the departments and organized into working committees. Except for Shriver and his assistant, Adam Yarmolinsky, the committee membership was informal and constantly changing. At one time or another Michael Harrington, Ylvisaker, Boone, Wilbur Cohen, Gordon, and Heller assisted Shriver.[77]

Shriver, whose main concern was the political appeal and effectiveness of the program,[78] was skeptical about the value and purpose of the CAPs. The day after his appointment was announced, he met with several of the individuals who had sponsored the community action idea. After hearing Heller, Gordon, Schultze, and William Capron, of the CEA staff, explain the idea, Shriver remarked that he could not see how it would work and, according to Capron, "from the very first saw this as one big headache."[79] When, several days later (on February 4), Secretary Wirtz appealed to the task force for more job-creating programs, Shriver agreed, saying that community action alone was insufficient. Shriver's assistant Yarmolinsky was also skeptical about the value of community action. Seeing community action as offering nothing more than a method of organization, he agreed with the departmental critics that single-purpose programs should be included in the legislation. At the February 4 meeting, a general consensus was reached to add single-purpose programs and cut back community action from $500 million to $300 million. During the first week, the task force added the Job Corps and the Neighborhood

76. Blumenthal, "The Bureaucracy," p. 158.
77. Sundquist, *Politics and Policy*, p. 142; Blumenthal, "The Bureaucracy," pp. 163–164.
78. Moynihan, "What Is Community Action?," *Public Interest* 3 (Fall 1966): 6.
79. Blumenthal, "The Bureaucracy," p. 164; Sundquist, *Politics and Policy*, p. 142.

Youth Corps, as well as various HEW community service proposals, Agriculture's loan and grant program, and adult training programs. During succeeding weeks a few new programs were added (e.g., VISTA) and an organization structure, the Office of Economic Opportunity, was developed. Title I of the bill was reserved for single-purpose programs. Community action was demoted to Title II.

The drafters of the actual wording of the legislation were two administration lawyers, Harold Horowitz, the associate general counsel of HEW, and Norbert Schlei, the assistant attorney general. Ambiguous sections of Title II (including Community Action Programs) would later be interpreted differently by different people. The ambiguities written into the legislation were not the sole fault of the drafters, however; the two attorneys were in frequent consultation with those previously involved in developing the community action idea, such as Cannon and Hackett. The fact was that these ambiguities had been present throughout the previous deliberations. The questions of CAPs' structure, jurisdiction, and composition had been repeatedly avoided. Many of those who had united to push for community action had differed from the beginning on the purposes of CAPs. Those individuals associated with the gray areas projects had seen these agencies as coordinating other institutions' efforts. Those associated with Mobilization for Youth, such as Cloward, had seen community action organization as a way for the poor to force institutional changes. While the first view saw the agency's purpose as building consensus, the latter saw it as producing conflict, so as, in the phrase of community action theorist Saul Alinsky, to "rub raw the sores of discontent."[80]

The provision that later created the greatest confusion and difficulty—as well as novelty— in the community action approach was the requirement that community action plans be "developed and conducted with the maximum feasible participation of the residents of the areas and members of groups" that would be affected by the program. Blumenthal traces the development of this provision:

> The member of the task force most responsible for the inclusion of the provision, though not its exact language, was Richard Boone. Officials at HEW wrote a pre-task force version that required Community Action

80. Moynihan, "What Is Community Action?," *Public Interest* 3 (Fall 1966): 5.

organizations to include representatives of neighborhood groups, but their aim was merely to prevent discrimination against Negroes in the South. Boone urged at the very first meeting that the task force take a much broader view of "involvement." "When you get a plan in an urban area," he told the others, "it may be just a plan among organizations . . . it may not *involve* the poor." As Boone repeated again and again the word "involvement," Yarmolinsky finally turned to him in exasperation, "How many times are you going to go on saying that?" Boone, unruffled, replied: "Until you put it in the legislation."

Still, there remains a touch of ominous mystery to the origin of the words "maximum" and "participation." Yarmolinsky attributes them to Boone, but Boone says "no, Norbert Schlei used them first." Schlei says his "only recollection is that [they] are in a rough, initial draft produced by Harold Horowitz." Moynihan, on the other hand, notes that "some suspicion points to Frank Mankiewicz," though "there is no proof."[81]

The rest of Title II was also vague. The community action program was to provide "services, assistance, and other activities . . . of sufficient variety, size, and scope to give promise of progress toward the elimination of poverty." There was no specification of geographical or political boundaries (although it was clearly intended for communities smaller than states). Both public and private nonprofit organizations were eligible as long as they were "broadly representative of the community."[82] The director of the program was given authority to prescribe additional requirements.

The bill was introduced in the House by the chairman of the Education and Labor Committee, Adam Clayton Powell, and by Senator Patrick McNamara of the Labor and Public Welfare Committee in the Senate. No member of Congress had been consulted or even briefed prior to the introduction of the legislation, and even the more interested congressmen understood only about "50 or 60 percent" of certain sections after the hearings. Blumenthal says:

> The fact is . . . that the objectives of Community Action were never resolved on the Hill. The theory of CAP was explored only superficially, and the "maximum feasible participation" clause was ignored entirely. . . . Most legislators not on the committee which dealt with the

81. Blumenthal, "The Bureaucracy," pp. 166–167. It is unclear to me how Mankiewicz, at the time an official of the Peace Corps, would have become involved.
82. Ibid., pp. 167–168.

bill—Education and Labor in the House, and Public Works and Labor [*sic*: actually Labor and Public Welfare] in the Senate—had only the vaguest notion of what CAP would mean in practice; and even many members of these committees now admit that they did not comprehend the type of activity Community Action would entail.[83]

Southern Democratic support was essential for passage of the legislation. Administration forces were fortunate in persuading Georgia Democrat Phil Landrum rather than the negligent Powell to manage the bill in the House.[84] Landrum was highly respected by his southern colleagues, and his influence was certain to have an impact on the final vote.[85] To placate the southerners, the administration accepted an amendment passed in each house to allow the governor of any state the power to veto any programs in his state not affiliated with institutions of higher learning.[86] Another amendment, allowing participation only of private groups (again excepting institutions of higher learning) that had already displayed a "concern" for poverty (a clause designed to eliminate the NAACP from eligibility) was also accepted by the bill's sponsors. In the House vote, the bill received the support of sixty of the hundred southern Democrats.[87] Despite these tactical concessions by the administration, the vote was close: 226 to 184. In the Senate, the outcome was never in doubt; it passed the legislation with few changes by a vote of 62 to 33.

83. Ibid., p. 169.

84. Sundquist, *Politics and Policy*, p. 149.

85. Landrum had been beaten in the Democratic caucus in January of the previous year for a Ways and Means seat and in hope of doing better the next time was showing a liberal face to his critics in the House. See Richard W. Bolling, *Defeating the Leadership's Nominee in the House Democratic Caucus*, Inter-University Case Program no. 91 (Indianapolis, Ind.: Bobbs-Merrill, 1965). Landrum got his Ways and Means seat in January 1965.

86. *Congressional Quarterly* (August 17, 1964): 1729–1730.

87. The bargaining over the bill was not altogether pleasant, as Evans and Novak describe it:

The subordination of all else to passage of the bill was tragically underscored in a kangaroo court held that week in Speaker McCormack's office. Adam Yarmolinsky, a liberal with impeccably anti-Communist credentials, had been the victim for years of an absurd but vicious right-wing smear painting him as a subversive and a security risk. This outrageous smear had seeped into the consciousness of conservative Congressmen. Now, on Thursday, August 6, in the privacy of

The CAP innovation was viewed by a number of influential groups as a favorable response to their own specialized and differing needs. President Johnson and the task force headed by Shriver saw the need in terms of a legislative package that would pass the Congress and provide a liberal record for the fall elections. Congressmen who were approached to support the bill gained vague impressions of public works funds to be distributed (perhaps with their influence) in their districts. The Budget Bureau saw the CAP proposal as merely an effective mechanism for the coordination of local poverty efforts; their concern was with efficiency, not political clout. For some of the planners involved in the Mobilization for Youth project, political efficacy was the goal: the CAPs could be used to produce more responsive local bureaucracies by encouraging conflict and confrontation with them. Still others saw the program as a means for providing better services for the poor and authentic experiences for the middle-class people who would offer those services.

As Moynihan has pointed out, many of these disparities in expectations about the ultimate aim of the project become clear only in retrospect. At the time, however, the different desires of all the involved groups tended to be subordinated to the common need for a money-dispensing organizational structure. CAPs fit this generalized need, while also appearing to meet many of the particular goals of each group. Ordinarily, such conflicts over the interpretation of a new policy would be settled in the process of enactment. Each position would find congressional champions, as, for example, in the case of the National Science Foundation, and the differences would

---

McCormack's office with Shriver present, conservative Democrats from North and South Carolina delivered an ultimatum: They would vote "no" on the crucial vote the next day unless they had absolute assurance that Yarmolinsky would be excluded from any part in administering the new program. . . . The Congressmen . . . insisted that a call be placed to Johnson. Shriver called the White House. He returned from the telephone to report: "The President has no objection to my saying that if I were appointed I would not recommend Yarmolinsky." Thus, an additional eight votes were secured—but at unpardonable cost to Yarmolinsky's reputation.
Rowland Evans and Robert Novak, *Lyndon B. Johnson: The Exercise of Power* (New York: New American Library, 1966), p. 432. See also Moynihan, *Maximum Feasible Misunderstanding*, p. 91.

be bargained out. But it did not happen that way in the case of the Community Action Programs, and one result was that the programs proved in some communities to be more innovative than many of their original supporters, in Congress and elsewhere, would have predicted.

No account of policy initiation in government is complete without at least one instance of policymaking by inadvertence. Accounts of the genesis of the maximum feasible participation clause are not notably confused about the intentions of some of the early champions of this innovation, but nevertheless a picture of misunderstandings, cross-purposes, and missed signals does emerge. It seems unlikely that maximum feasible participation would have survived careful scrutiny by President Johnson, by Congress, or by the Budget Bureau if any of these had paid close attention to this feature of the bill. But none did. Here, as in the case of civilian control of atomic energy, the key to policy innovation was the presence within the government of policy entrepreneurs, persons who knew whatever there was to know about programs in the area, with ideas of their own and opportunities to write these ideas into the law of the land. And like the case of civilian control of atomic energy, the President at first paid little or no attention to presidential stakes in the outcome. Harry Truman eventually focused on the problem of civilian control long enough to protect his interests; Lyndon Johnson in the case of the Community Action Programs evidently never did. It was Johnson and his desire for a big splash that created the omnibus bill, scaled pilot projects up into a much larger commitment, and hustled the proposal through Congress without careful consultation.

Where did the need for legislation on poverty come from? Perhaps it was the result of something as ephemeral as a mood in official Washington that was evoked by the great popularity of Michael Harrington's book on poverty, and the knowledge that the book had touched President Kennedy. The general level of prosperity in the nation must have played a part, since it encouraged administration economists to address the problem of structural unemployment— normally not a central concern when the state of the economy is less buoyant. Finally, there was the insatiable urge of President Johnson for tangible accomplishment, and lopsided Democratic majorities in

Congress available to gratify that urge—if the bill could be readied in time for the Eighty-ninth Congress.

Thus, like the emergency surrounding civilian control of atomic energy, the legislative timetable for community action built in a certain amount of haste, leading to intense bargaining within the government and the acceptance by all participants of severe time constraints.

V

Innovations Compared

1. TYPES OF POLICY INITIATION

The question now arises whether we can tease out of the instances of policy initiation we have so far considered a few general propositions about the process of innovation in American politics. We may dispose at once, I think, of the classification scheme implicit in the organization of the last three chapters, that is, by general subject matter. Within each of the three categories—science policy, foreign policy, and domestic policy—there was enough substantive variation, and in some cases even contrast, to suggest first that subject matter alone does not conclusively determine the process by which policy is initiated and, second, that the agencies that characteristically process each subject, while they may be more hospitable to approaches from one source than another, are nevertheless susceptible to initiation by more than one means.

The two cases classified under "foreign policy" will serve to make this point, since of all the policy areas of American government, this one is commonly held to be the most uniformly resistant to innovation, and the most closely managed by a circumscribed elite. One initiation, the Truman Doctrine, was indeed the product of the activity of a governmental elite, buttressed by staff work in "normal channels" and legitimized by top-level consultation with Congress.[1]

In contrast, the Peace Corps seems to have emerged almost by

1. Herbert Feis, quasi-official historian of the diplomacy of the period, says much the same of the Marshall Plan, which followed swiftly on the heels of the Truman Doctrine:

the account in the memoirs of the emergence and introduction of the Marshall Plan, like all other official versions, is historically foreshortened. It was not a sudden bolt of initiative launched by a few farsighted top officials. The American

accident, bubbling up from a number of sources, but certainly not in response to a pressing need identified by an alert governmental agency. If we add to these two cases the account of the nuclear test ban, it seems to me difficult to argue that there is something about foreign policy innovation as a process or activity that plausibly groups these cases together and separates them from policy initiation in other subject areas. In fact, the seven dimensions of the policy initiation process that have served us in organizing the case materials and comparing and contrasting two or more cases so far are better suited to a preliminary taxonomy of political innovation.

For the purposes of hypothesis finding, such as engage us here, it does not make much sense to be long detained by the problem of establishing and justifying a fastidious scheme of measurement with respect to each of these dimensions. I propose to regard each of the seven dimensions as in principle continuous, and capable of yielding quantitative estimates for each of the cases. For convenience, we can break each continuum into three parts, thus yielding a fairly compact classification scheme along seven dimensions on which we can place each of our eight cases. In table 5.1 the cases are arrayed according to this scheme.

---

government had failed to perceive the severity and depth of the exhaustion of our former allies, and to foresee that they would not be able to recuperate and become self-sustaining without ample and continued help. It had been slow to recognize that the prescriptions of [Secretary of State Cordell] Hull, Will Clayton [who was Assistant, then Undersecretary, for Economic Affairs during this period], and their acolytes could not produce recovery until the economic system of these nations was strengthened.

The corrective response was evoked first by ominous reports sent in by our foreign missions, and the grim analyses contained in the memos written by junior economists and political officers. Their warnings of the impending collapse of the economies of Western Europe and of possible social disorders aroused alarm which routed complacence. Even Clayton, the doctrinaire, while on a mission in Europe became so worried that he ceased to reckon cost more than consequence, and to admit the need for special infusion of aid.

In a speech in Mississippi, Acheson first undertook to reveal this deepening impression to the country and Congress. Thereafter many talents contributed energy, will, and innovative ideas to formulate what became Secretary Marshall's proposal. His sponsorship was its credential, needed to move the cautious, the stubbornly dubious, the guardians of the budget.

Herbert Feis, "Memoirs of State," *Yale Review* 59 (March 1970): 401.

Table 5.1. Comparing Political Innovations

Timing

Fast		*Slow*
Civilian Control of Atomic Energy	National Science Foundation	Medicare
Community Action Programs	Peace Corps	Council of Economic Advisers
Truman Doctrine		Nuclear Test Ban Treaty

Specialization

Experts very influential, not elected officials or politicians		*Politicians, elected officials very influential, not experts*
Civilian Control	Medicare	Truman Doctrine
Community Action Programs	Peace Corps	
NSF	Test Ban	
CEA		

Subculture

High early agreement about the need to act		*No early agreement about the need to act*
Truman Doctrine	Civilian Control	Community Action Programs
NSF		Medicare
		Peace Corps
		CEA
		Test Ban

Saliency

Alternatives publicized widely before the enactment phase		*Alternatives not widely publicized to general public*
Civilian Control	Truman Doctrine	Community Action Programs
Medicare	Peace Corps	NSF
Nuclear Test Ban		CEA

NOTE: A word is in order on the coding procedure that produced the arrays visible in this table. As will be apparent, this procedure occupies a methodological limbo somewhere between the sheerly arbitrary assignment of cases to categories by the

Table 5.1.	Comparing Political Innovations	*(continued)*

Political Conflict

Strong and opposed party positions on the issue	←——————————→	*Not much disagreement between parties*
Medicare	Test Ban	Civilian Control
Peace Corps		Community Action
CEA		Programs
		NSF
		Truman Doctrine

Research

Researched solutions	←——————————→	*Improvised solutions*
Medicare	NSF	Civilian Control
Test Ban	Peace Corps	Community Action
	CEA	Programs
		Truman Doctrine

Staging

Invention of alternatives separate from process of search	←——————————→	*Processes of invention and search unified*
Medicare	NSF	Civilian Control
Peace Corps		Community Action
CEA		Programs
		Truman Doctrine
		Test Ban

author and the automated splendor of a precoded forced-choice questionnaire. The cases were classified in the following manner. Fourteen graduate students in political science at Berkeley read the case materials and were asked independently to fill in the table—that is, to rate each case low, medium, or high with respect to each variable. We then met in seminar and aggregated our findings. There were very few disagreements; where these occurred, a consensus rating was battled out by a process that included examining justifications for individual choices, splitting differences, and voting. Thus this table is meant to be a shorthand reflection of the case studies. There is bound to be a residual looseness about this table, however. The seven dimensions are not perfectly well bounded and singular in the behavior to which they refer. This affects not only the integrity of the vertical classification, but also reproducibility along the horizontal axis. I acknowledge all this for the record, in the spirit of one who, hacking his way through unmapped territory, confesses that he is not providing a four-lane highway for those who follow in his path. I believe that adequate precautions were taken against arbitrariness, but readers may appropriately retain a measure of skepticism.

The table permits a number of observations. First, two methodological points. There is some variation among cases with respect to each dimension. No dimension is so uninteresting as to fail to produce some differences among the eight cases studied. Likewise, no two dimensions appear to be merely different names for the same thing. In no instances do ratings on any two dimensions fall in exactly the same way for all eight cases. Whether these dimensions prove substantively interesting is another matter. We can, however, begin to explore this question reasonably confident that the variables we have initially chosen to examine do vary and do distinguish among our cases.

Three cases—civilian control of atomic energy, Community Action Programs, and the Truman Doctrine—cluster on four dimensions. In this cluster, which I shall refer to as type A or "acute" innovation, the lapse in time between the first surfacing of an idea within the subculture of decision-makers and its enactment is short. The sources of ideas under such circumstances are people relatively close to the agencies ultimately responsible for enactment, and there is little time or effort expended on research. In the case of the Truman Doctrine, General Eisenhower's proposal for a comprehensive survey was explicitly short-circuited. In Community Action, more than a little difficulty resulted from the subsequent realization on the part of many actors that they had not anticipated the consequences of maximum feasible participation. In the case of civilian control of atomic energy, alternatives were so little thought out or deliberated that the principal decision-maker, the President, changed sides in midstream. For type A innovation, the invention of alternatives is part of the process of search. Policies actually enacted are likely to reflect the circumstances under which search is conducted. Not all feasible or likely alternatives are canvassed. The first alternative hit upon that satisfies minimal criteria of tension reduction or problem abatement is likely to be chosen.[2] The decision-making process for type

2. Thus the more like type A an innovation is, the more likely actors will promptly "satisfice," in the useful terminology of Herbert A. Simon. See Simon, "A Behavioral Model of Rational Choice," in *Models of Man: Social and Rational* (New York: John Wiley and Sons, 1957), pp. 241–260.

A innovation thus resembles the "organized anarchy" of decision theorists.[3]

In type A innovation, whoever comes to the right meeting, or happens to have done his homework, or has the loudest voice on a particular occasion, may carry the day. Whoever put the words "maximum feasible participation" into the community action legislation seems to have done his work so unobtrusively that a few years after the event, nobody is quite sure who did it or how it was done. For the Truman Doctrine, the voices of Dean Acheson and Arthur Vandenberg seem to have been crucial, first in fixing the character of the problem, and then in promoting the alternative finally chosen. In the atomic energy case Vandenberg was again significant in assuring that form would influence substance, by shunting matters off to a special Senate committee, where the jurisdictional battle for congressional oversight could be contested rather than automatically resolved against him.

The main lines of conflict in the atomic energy case were not partisan but jurisdictional; congressional committees fought for a piece of the action on one level, and scientific bureaucrats squared off against military-science bureaucrats on another. Type A innovation is characterized by this sort of relatively truncated and contained conflict, where justifications are relatively free of partisan ideology and of the sort of rhetoric more suited to the persuasion of mass audiences. The Truman Doctrine is of course the clearest case of this, where spokesmen of both major parties were explicitly mobilized behind the chosen alternative before it was given publicity. Curiously, partisan conflict was also absent from the maximum feasible participation case, where an improvised idea, potentially full of political mischief, simply went through the enactment process without exciting partisan notice.

It is premature to state that the four characteristics that hang together in these three cases—low partisan conflict, minimal re-

3. See Michael D. Cohen, James G. March and Johan P. Olsen, "A Garbage-Can Model of Organizational Choice," *Administrative Science Quarterly* 17 (March 1972): 1–25. Properties of "organized anarchies" include problematic preferences, unclear technology, and fluid participation.

search, short elapsed time, and fusion of stages—are either necessary or sufficient conditions of type A innovation. Logically, one would assume that these four characteristics would also cluster with the variable we have referred to as great consensus within the subculture of decision-makers. When time—or the subjective perception of available time by decision-makers—is short and political actors are being pressed to search for alternatives, and partisanship is low and it is too late for research, one would assume that leaders would be in general agreement about what the "problem" is. But real life cases do not necessarily conform to ideal types. There was this sort of agreement in the case of the Truman Doctrine, but not in the other two cases. For Community Action there was no widespread sense that a problem even existed; with civilian control there was considerable disagreement among leaders about what the problem was until the Hiroshima bomb went off.

These three cases also differentiated rather than clustered along the specialization dimension. For the Truman Doctrine, politicians and high-ranking officials were predominantly involved; in the other two cases, "experts" and "specialists" were extremely important. The ubiquitous James Newman in the atomic energy case is perhaps as good an example as exists in the annals of modern American government of an expert being on top and not just on tap. And it was assuredly not politicians who invented maximum feasible participation.[4]

Finally, the three type A cases range all over the spectrum with respect to the public saliency of their emergence; Community Action was done in the dark of night, civilian control in the high noon of public awareness, and the Truman Doctrine, though fairly thoroughly publicized, was really decided on before it was advertised to the public.

Another cluster of cases—Medicare, the Peace Corps, and the Council of Economic Advisers—emerges from our classification

4. Senator Daniel Patrick Moynihan, himself a social scientist, fulminates with particular vividness on this point. See *Maximum Feasible Misunderstanding: Community Action in the war on poverty* (New York: Free Press, 1969), pp. 167–205 passim. For a more measured view of the war on poverty and of the role of experts, see Henry Aaron, *Politics and the Professors* (Washington, D.C.: Brookings Institution, 1978), especially pp. 16–64.

scheme; let us call this cluster type B or "incubated" innovation. Type B innovation takes place slowly, frequently over many years. As was also true of one of the three type A innovations, there is no early widespread consensus on the need for action on the problem to which the innovation is addressed. Indeed there is at first no widespread acknowledgment of the existence of a problem. Type B innovations are not introduced surreptitiously like Community Action Programs, or as a side issue, like civilian control of atomic energy. Rather the demand for innovation is built slowly, and specific plans or proposals are typically the work of people relatively far in social, temporal, and sometimes physical distance from ultimate decision-makers: experts and researchers working in universities or in quasi-academic settings, or technical staff employees of interest groups, government agencies, or congressional committees. These innovations pass through a stage of *incubation*, where political actors—senators, congressmen, lobbyists, or other promoters—take the idea up, reshape it, adapt it to their political needs, publicize it, and put it into the ongoing culture of decision-makers. This culture endures in Washington and in national politics, maintaining an interest in various subject areas from generation to generation and assimilating new participants as they drift into town with the tides of electoral politics.[5]

Incubated innovations as proposals often find their way into partisan politics, into national party platforms and senatorial speeches, and as controverted items at congressional hearings. Medicare, for example, was part of the Democratic program for many years, while Republicans frequently attacked it as socialized medicine. The Peace Corps emerged in the context not of a governmental need but of a

---

5. My article "The Washington Community, 1960–1980" in Thomas E. Mann and Norman J. Ornstein, eds., *The New Congress* (Washington, D.C.: American Enterprise Institute, 1981), pp. 7–31, discusses this enduring culture in some detail. In *Power in Washington*, (New York: Random House, 1964), Douglass Cater refers to issue-specific groups in Washington that endure over time as "subgovernments"; see especially pp. 26–48. J. Leiper Freeman in *The Political Process: Executive Bureau-Legislative Committee Relations* (Garden City, N.Y.: Doubleday, 1955) treats these groups as "policy subsystems." And Hugh Heclo much more recently adopts the term "issue networks" to refer to roughly the same thing. See Heclo, "Issue Networks and the Executive Establishment," in Anthony King, ed., *The New American Political System* (Washington, D.C.: American Enterprise Institute, 1978), pp. 87–124.

presidential candidate's campaign speech and was accordingly attacked by the other side. And the Council of Economic Advisers was debated when it was first proposed in the context of a larger ideological controversy over the efficacy—and appropriateness for the United States—of "planning."

As type B innovations gather patrons, so they gain the notice of enemies. Thus the scope of conflict surrounding type B innovation is relatively wide. Where type A innovations are often jerry-built, improvised and hasty, type B innovations are often founded upon much research and reasoned advocacy. This was certainly the case with respect to Medicare, where enactment would have been very difficult without comprehensive analyses of the consequences of varying types and levels of benefits and thorough exploration of the implications of financing through the Social Security system. The Council of Economic Advisers idea had had a long life in the research and policy analysis community before it was brought forward for enactment. Before the Peace Corps was formed it became the subject of systematic research, by a bona fide research organization as well as one or two task forces, since the idea as President Kennedy had expressed it had little substance. It is striking to recall that the financing of this research was actually provided for by a process that was entirely separate from the process that propelled the Peace Corps toward enactment.

In this, one also sees the final characteristic of type B innovation: a lag between the proposal of alternatives and the search by the system for solutions to problems to which these alternatives are addressed. Where policy proposals are "in the air" for a period of time before the system begins to search for solutions to the problem to which they refer, as in the type B cases, it is much more likely that a canvass of alternatives is conducted, that longer-range consequences are considered, and that more elaborate justifications and projections are demanded by decision-makers. These are necessary to ward off opponents and can be feasibly undertaken because the activities of proponents over long periods of time creates an intellectual residue that can be pressed into service.

An implication of the presence of research when the innovation is long, drawn out, and controverted, and the absence of research when innovations are quick and uncontroverted, is that one condition

normally assumed for socially relevant research to take place—
namely, an absence of controversy, which permits a continuity of
effort regardless of political changes—is probably neither necessary
nor sufficient. It may in fact be the case that the opposite state of
affairs (i.e., controversy) is a necessary condition of research since it,
not lack of controversy, provides the time that is essential for technical competence to weigh in decision-making. When there is no
conflict over whether something must be done, "something" may be
done too quickly for research and technical competence to affect
decision-making or the choice of alternatives.

Thus a major cause of research in policy innovation appears to be
controversy. This finding reverses the conventional wisdom, which
associates systematic search, the conscientious relating of means to
ends, the consideration of alternatives, and the testing of alternatives
against goals with the plodding, uncontentious routines of hierarchical decision-making.[6] Evidently all these activities are a part of policy
initiation only when the decision-making structure is not hierarchical
but multicentered, and moreover when occupants of the various
centers of power are in sharp disagreement over preferred outcomes.

There is no exact correspondence in content between the alternatives that waited in the wings and the provisions of the eventual
enactment in the Medicare and Council of Economic Advisers cases.
Over the years, proposals for Medicare coverage swelled and shrank
as prospects for enactment changed and alternative schemes for
financing the project hove into view. The notion of a CEA changed
over the years from a control instrument of the corporate state via
comprehensive interest-group representation to a statistical service
bureau, and then to a central agency of presidential fiscal planning, as
certain branches of economic theory grew in their ambitions and
capacities to deal with the real world.

How, then, do we allocate responsibility for an "eventual" outcome between actors who appear early and those who appear late in
the life of an issue? Consider the following:

1. Machinery for an internal security program was developed and
   put into effect by the Roosevelt and Truman administrations.

6. See Charles E. Lindblom, "The Science of Muddling Through," *Public Administration Review* 19 (Spring 1959): 79–88.

The Eisenhower administration, invoking this machinery, though using somewhat different criteria, denied a security clearance to J. Robert Oppenheimer. Who "caused" the Oppenheimer case?[7]

2. Commitments of some sort or other toward governments in Indochina had been made by the administrations of Presidents Eisenhower and Kennedy. President Johnson increased these commitments, always describing his acts as continuing and logically extending prior American commitments. Who "caused" the condition that later came to be defined as American overcommitment in Vietnam?[8]

In common sense and ordinary conversation it is not difficult to allocate "responsibility" for later acts to later actors. "Responsibility" entails not merely accountability under constitutional processes, but also a shared perception that alternative courses of action are avail-

---

7. Philip M. Stern, *The Oppenheimer Case* (New York: Harper and Row, 1969). See also Athan Theoharis, *Seeds of Repression: Harry S. Truman and the Origins of McCarthyism* (Chicago: Quadrangle, 1971), and Richard M. Freeland, *The Truman Doctrine and the Origins of McCarthyism* (New York: Knopf, 1972), who argue that the Truman administration, by having a loyalty-security program and "scaring hell out of the country" at the time of the establishment of the Truman Doctrine, legitimized claims about the seriousness of the issue of internal subversion and therefore "caused" McCarthyism. Or, as Freeland says:
[T]he emotional and political forces and the patterns of belief—what in aggregate might be called the "Cold War consensus"—that were to provide the essential energies of postwar anti-communism were quite fully developed by early 1948 . . . . These emotions were aroused and these patterns of belief developed, it is argued, as the result of a deliberate and highly organized effort by the Truman administration in 1947–8 to mobilize support for the program of economic assistance to Europe called the European Recovery Program, or Marshall Plan. In the absence of this Cold War consensus, it seems likely that the events that triggered McCarthyism would have been accepted with relative calm. Thus it is the campaign for foreign aid that must be analyzed if the inevitability of McCarthyism is to be assessed (p. 5).
8. There are many and greatly varied answers to this question. See Leslie H. Gelb and Richard Betts, *The Irony of Vietnam: The System Worked* (Washington, D.C.: Brookings Institution, 1979); Guenter Lewy, *American in Vietnam* (New York: Oxford University Press, 1978); David Halberstam, *The Making of a Quagmire* (New York: Random House, 1965), especially pp. 33ff.; Norman Podhoretz, *Why We Were in Vietnam* (New York: Simon and Schuster, 1982), pp. 16–63; and Noam Chomsky, *American Power and the New Mandarins* (New York: Pantheon, 1967), pp. 24–28.

able to later actors even given the constraints imposed by the previous actions of earlier actors. Without these options, later actors cannot properly be held to account, since they would be able to claim that they were unable to control their own behavior.

When alternatives for later actors exist, does it make sense to trace "responsibility" for Medicare back to the early part of the twentieth century rather than assigning "credit" to Wilbur Mills, for example? In my opinion, two senses of the word "responsibility" cause this question to occur. Moral or political responsibility, credit or blame, can be assessed against adults having options, so long as they can reasonably be expected to perceive that alternatives exist, even when they are not personally responsible for having created all the alternatives—or the most attractive alternatives, or the most likely to be chosen alternatives—available to them. [9] If the question, however, is one not of assessing moral responsibility or granting political credit, but of understanding the complex processes that account for the origins of social behavior and political choices, then attentiveness to historical continuities, to institutional habits and constraints, is not only tenable but necessary.

Thus it is far from nonsense to claim that alternatives finally chosen would never have come to the attention of decision-makers had not the precursors and collateral cousins of these alternatives existed and repeatedly been brought forward into the political arena. Elite policymaking in any complex society is of necessity in some large measure a battle among small groups of people who have interests and information for the attention of constitutionally responsible and politically visible elites. If an "issue" does not exist, if alternative solutions are not devised in the first place, then it is hard to see how the attention can be gained of an advocate, of some decision-maker who can bring political or organizational resources to bear upon the complicated and difficult tasks of focusing the decision-making apparatus of government. This latter activity is the central vocation of decision-makers; giving them something substantively worthwhile to

9. Thus I think that the Theoharis-Freeland argument, insofar as it attempts to fix moral or political responsibility for McCarthyism on the Truman administration, is without merit. There is also the issue of the proper weight to be given to the influence of leaders of the Republican party who supported McCarthy rather than opposing him, as President Truman did.

do is yet another specialty, that of the policy entrepreneur, examples of which we have encountered.

It is in incubated innovation that the specialized tasks of policy entrepreneurs, as contrasted with those of political decision-makers, are most apparent, since each characteristically operates at a different stage of the type B innovation process, whereas they are likely to coexist at the same stage in the acute innovation process.

Although four attributes of decision-making appear to cause these cases to form clusters, three do not. The eight cases vary all over the lot, for example, with respect to saliency: civilian control (type A), Medicare (type B), and the nuclear test ban treaty (no type) enjoyed enormous general publicity before and during their enactment; the Truman Doctrine (type A) and the Peace Corps (type B) fall somewhere in the middle; and the remaining three cases, Community Action Programs (type A), the Council of Economic Advisers (type B),

Table 5.2.   Types of Innovations

Acute (Type A) (Civilian Control, Truman Doctrine, Community Action)	Incubated (Type B) (Medicare, Peace Corps, Council of Economic Advisers)
Timing	
Short lapse of time between idea and enactment.	Innovation slow, frequently over many years. Demand for innovation built slowly.
Research	
Little time or energy devoted to research on alternatives.	Alternatives systematically justified by recourse to formally assembled facts and figures.
Staging	
Alternative is invented during search process, with first good one chosen: fusion of stages and "satisficing."	Separation between proposal of alternatives and search by system for solutions to problems to which alternatives are addressed. Systematic canvass of alternatives.
Conflict	
Truncated and constrained. Justifications free of ideology or mass-appeal elements. Low partisanship.	Strong and opposed party positions. Ideological justifications and attacks (e.g., "socialized medicine"; "government planning").

and the National Science Foundation (no type) fall on the low end of
the scale, generating little or no publicity or coming to notice only
within the "publics" created by narrowly bounded interest groups.

Likewise, the participation of specialists does not differentiate the
clusters, and the reason seems to be that experts are nearly every-
where; only in the Truman Doctrine case were they virtually absent
from the process that selected and justified alternatives. In four
cases, distributed between and outside our two main types, specialists were extremely important, and in three, they shared with politicians in the process of selecting alternatives.

Finally, the existence of a united and consensual decision-making
subculture fails to distinguish our types for the opposite reason: a
fairly unified set of intellectual coordinates upon which bargaining
about details can rest turns out to be unusual. Our most frequent
finding—in five cases out of eight—is, to the contrary, that on the
whole decision-makers do not agree about whether problems exist,
and hence whether "solutions" are necessary. Decision-makers turn
out to be widely scattered in their patterns of attentiveness. Thus
type A innovation consists of letting sleeping dogs lie and slipping an
initiation by as a side issue or as a nonissue; type B innovation consists
of meeting opposition head-on and overcoming it.

I have remarked that some of our dimensions of decision-making
failed to differentiate between our main types of innovation. In
addition, two of the cases we studied—the National Science Foundation and the nuclear test ban treaty—failed to fit into either of our
clusters, and each failed in a different way. This should occasion no
surprise, except to those who believe the world is a very simple place.
It is likely that there are more than two main types of innovation
process in the American political system and yet, as our investigation
so far suggests, fewer such processes than there are discrete cases of
policy initiation.

2. WHAT CAUSES INNOVATION?

Each of the case accounts testifies to a powerful underlying cluster of
cultural norms and biases that, I believe, make policy initiation
possible. These can be variously described as a widely shared belief
in the malleability of the world, as a belief that there are such things

as causes that have effects, and that, when changed, have different effects, and as a belief that outcomes that have meanings in people's lives can by political effort be evoked, modulated, and deflected.

It is tempting to refer to such a cluster of beliefs as "innovation-prone" and to draw a contrast with underlying cultural beliefs that discourage innovation. Such beliefs would be found, for example, in societies in which it is customary to discern only weak linkages between earthbound causes and effects; in which leaders take a pessimistic view of their efficacy in directly manipulating the world; in which leaders are required to adhere strictly to rituals; in which a high value is placed upon the maintenance of ancestral or traditional ways; or in which social and political life is organized around affirmations of harmonious acquiescence to forces larger than the individual or the contemporary mores of the social group.[10]

I do not suggest that in such settings innovation is utterly impossible; in fact, one may conjecture that if such a society is able to achieve stability and order within its boundaries, and economic surplus, great intellectual or artistic energy might well be released. Here, however, we are concerned with political and social innovation, rather than the elaboration of traditional artistic forms.

A limiting case on the other side of the spectrum is the revolutionary society, in which social upheaval is the norm. Here, clearly, faith in the capacity of individuals to change their collective fate reaches a high point. Moreover, revolutions may legitimately be said to cause policy innovation of all kinds. And so it is formally tenable to say that one assured path to political innovation lies through revolution. Our cases may suggest, however, that making revolution is a hard—even an expensive—way to innovate, since the existence of innovation-prone underlying beliefs does not seem necessarily to coincide with a disposition to rebel against the entire fabric of society.

10. The attitudes and values contrasted here have frequently been invoked in social analysis. See, for a famous example, Max Weber's *The Protestant Ethic and the Spirit of Capitalism* (New York: Scribner, 1930) and *Economy and Society*, ed. Guenther Roth and Claus Wittich (Berkeley and Los Angeles: University of California Press, 1978), passim. Or, more recently, Everett M. Rogers, *Diffusion of Innovations* (New York: Free Press of Glencoe, 1962); and John H. Sims and Duane D. Baumann, "The Tornado Threat: Coping Styles of the North and South," *Science* 176 (June 30, 1972): 1386–1392.

Oddly enough, what our cases do seem to show is that the parts of the American political system that have come under our scrutiny—institutions by no means contributing to the revolutionary potential of the society—routinely create needs and tensions that frequently are resolved by recourse to the policy innovation process. Among these routine stimuli to innovation one can identify, for example, the fact that Presidents must have programs. A central part of the regular quadrennial public competition for the presidential office is that candidates must display a willingness to grapple with human needs, and incumbents, if they care either for reelection or for the kindly verdict of history, must find programs to which they can attach their names and from which they can hope to extract a little credit.

Two innovations—Medicare and the Peace Corps—constitute good illustrations of innovations inspired or sustained by the needs generated by political routines. Without the necessity to come up with a program, it is doubtful that Democratic Presidents would repeatedly over the years have made Medicare an issue. And for the Peace Corps, a presidential campaign—a predictable quadrennial event—provided the fertile ground on which long-ready seeds could fall.

We can count on the calendar producing a presidential election campaign every four years, and with it, needs on both sides and by all prospective candidates for policies and programs; this is one reason that leaders routinely search for policy alternatives. Prospective candidates search for issues with which they can become identified, for themes that will resonate with national constituencies. These themes provide a means for quick and favorable identification with electorates that can help candidates realize their ambitions. A second routine we have identified as principally affecting Presidents, but it also affects all those Washington political actors who wish to define themselves in some measure in terms of policy. Presidents who wish to differentiate themselves from their predecessors and who want to make an individual mark on history—as nearly all do—provide a steady market for policy innovations.[11]

So also do other political actors who see policy as one important means of public self-definition, and as a way of nurturing ambitions

11. This chronic presidential need brings problems as well as innovations in its train. See my "Against Presidential Greatness," *Commentary* 63 (January 1977): 61–64, for a brief discussion.

for higher office. This is nowadays especially noticeable in the Senate, where increasingly the national media of publicity have focused. In our cases, Vandenberg on civilian control and the Truman Doctrine, Humphrey on the nuclear test ban and the Peace Corps—both sometime presidential hopefuls in their respective parties—were notably active and entrepreneurial. Indeed in some respects Vandenberg invented, and Humphrey elaborated in an especially creative way, the role of the modern senator in what in their time was a modernizing Senate.[12]

One commandment of Senate life left over from the premodern days, when norms of internal service governed the place, is that senators "specialized."[13] When the life of the Senate was turned predominantly inward, this norm had obvious advantages in strengthening the division of labor. Observable in our cases, however, are indications that during the 1950s, specialization had begun to take on an expanded meaning for senators.

In the modern Senate the three central activities are (1) the cultivation of national constituencies by political leaders; (2) the formulation of questions for debate and discussion on a national scale, especially in opposition to the President; and (3) the incubation of new policy proposals that may at some future time find their way into legislation.[14] To succeed as a senator or to enhance his political future, a senator must develop a reputation for competence, a set of policy specializations, and ties to national constituencies beyond the bounds of a single state.[15] The division of labor in the Senate is not highly

12. For more on the modernization of the Senate see my "Goodbye to the Inner Club," in Nelson W. Polsby, ed., *Congressional Behavior* (New York: Random House, 1971), pp. 105–110; Michael Foley, *The New Senate: Liberal Influence on a Conservative Institution, 1959–1972* (New Haven: Yale University Press, 1980); and Jack L. Walker, "Setting the Agenda in the U.S. Senate: A Theory of Problem-Selection," *British Journal of Political Science* 7 (October 1977): 423–445.

13. See Donald R. Matthews, "The Folkways of the U.S. Senate," *American Political Science Review* 53 (December 1959): 1064–1089; and *U.S. Senators and Their World* (Chapel Hill, N.C.: University of North Carolina Press, 1960).

14. See my "Strengthening Congress in National Policy-Making," in *Congressional Behavior*, pp. 3–13.

15. David Price is explicit in linking policy entrepreneurship on the part of Senate staff with the political ambitions of senators: "[T]he fact that the development of policy

structured; while it rewards specialization, it provides few cues and fewer compulsions to specialize in any particular mode. So senators must search for ways to specialize on their own. Above all, from the standpoint of national policymaking, the Senate is a great forum. Occasionally this forum serves as the arena for the debate of grave national issues. But, more often by far, this forum is nothing more or less than a gigantic echo chamber, a publicity machine that publicizes things that individual senators want publicized. As nature abhors a vacuum, so do politicians abhor a silent echo chamber; this has given senators an opportunity to make of the Senate an incubator of policy innovation in the American system.

This is less true of the House, primarily because of its stricter division of labor, its restrictions on debate, and its greater mass of members, who thus enjoy less notoriety. Hence the House is structurally less hospitable to the hobbies and fancies of individual members, no matter how meaningful and constructive they are.[16] Even so, from time to time, a member or a subcommittee finds a niche from which it can incubate policy innovation. Frequently a congressman so engaged finds himself running for higher office soon after. It is primarily and most often the Senate that is at this crucial nerve end of the polity; it articulates, formulates, shapes, and publicizes demands and can serve as a hothouse for significant policy innovation.

The nuclear test ban is one case in which members of Congress took major steps to keep an idea viable before the enactment phase. The Peace Corps is another. They can be contrasted with instances in which congressional roles were more closely tied to enactment, such as the cases of Representative Whittington and the Council of Economic Advisers and Representative Mills and Medicare. In the latter

---

and the promotion of [Senator Warren] Magnuson were seen by staff and chairman alike as two sides of the same coin undoubtedly provided motivation and a focus for effort." David E. Price, "Professionals and Entrepreneurs: Staff Orientations and Policy Making on Three Senate Committees," *Journal of Politics* 33 (May 1971): 325.

16. Thus Representative Henry Reuss in the nature of things could get less political mileage from his Peace Corps initiative than Senator Hubert Humphrey could from his. When the Peace Corps bill went into its enactment stage, the Senate bill was Humphrey's bill; the House sponsor had to be the chairman of the Foreign Affairs Committee, Dr. Thomas Morgan, not Reuss.

cases, we can observe congressmen trafficking in power: they were after immediate results and the packages they put together were meant to emerge promptly as laws. To be sure, policy alternatives that can meet this test are always welcome on Capitol Hill. I want to draw attention, however, to another set of transactions, the career-long alliances that elective officials build with interest groups within a subject area, and the processes by which the preferences of one become the preoccupations of both. This entails, on the side of the legislator, proposing bills that may or may not have a chance of immediate enactment, but which provide an occasion for a speech or two or a hearing at which interest-group advocates have their say.

This relationship is a two-way street. As senators and congressmen become champions of labor or of the farmers, or advocates of disarmament, of education, or of the civil service, they also learn about the substance of policy that concerns these national constituencies. And they frequently carry these old loyalties along with them as they seek higher office. [17]

A final routine source of stimuli to innovation is the organizational needs of bureaucracies. The civilian control of atomic energy case started with a scientific laboratory threatened with extinction. As the laboratory searched for ways to remain useful, it began also to seek to innovate and to invent new policies. It is not uncommon to hear of such a sequence of events.

Several authoritative commentators, for example, have shown how innovations in strategic doctrines concerning the defense of the United States were directly tied to rivalry among the armed services in the post−World War II period. Samuel P. Huntington says:

> The sensitivity of military groups to new program needs depends largely upon service doctrine and service interests. The Air Force was active in pushing strategic deterrence and the Army in innovating European defense since each program was closely related to existing service doctrine. [18]

17. This conception of senatorial effectiveness is of course greatly at odds with the notion in Matthews, *U.S. Senators and Their World*, pp. 277−278, of effectiveness measured by the sponsorship of bills that are promptly enacted.
18. Samuel P. Huntington, *The Common Defense* (New York: Columbia University Press, 1961), p. 288.

Michael Armacost agrees:

> Naturally the rate and direction of technological innovation is condi-
> tioned by the strategic perspectives and proprietary interests of the
> services.[19]

To the question "What causes innovation?" we have thus far given
two answers: first, an underlying cultural disposition must be present favoring the application of rational thought to problems; second,
the political system must embody incentives to search for innovations. Both these conditions are clearly met in the American political
system; indeed, I have suggested that the second condition is incorporated into the constitutional routines of the American political
process as they affect the ambitions of politicians—routines associated with the electoral cycle and routines associated with the separation of powers.

Even when leaders believe that in their environment there are
"problems" that can be "solved," and when there are built-in
systemic incentives to search for solutions, the actual solutions
themselves must come from somewhere. A system that provides no
mechanisms for the actual invention of alternatives and for their
communication to decision-makers is unlikely to innovate.

In fact, these cases do provide evidence on the process of invention
as well, the process that in the first instance causes alternatives to
come into existence. As a matter of intellectual history, policy innova-

19. Michael H. Armacost, *The Politics of Weapons Innovation* (New York: Columbia University Press, 1969), p. 6. See, in general, Huntington, *The Common Defense*,
pp. 284–368; Edmund Beard, *Developing the ICBM* (New York: Columbia University Press, 1976); and Vincent Davis, *The Politics of Innovation: Patterns in Navy
Cases*, Monograph Series in World Affairs, vol. 4, no. 3 (Denver: Social Science
Foundation and Graduate School of International Studies, University of Denver,
1966–67). Interservice rivalry continues to stimulate and winnow policy innovations.
Here is a recent example, on the subject of the basing of guided missiles: "Despite an
aggressive sales campaign, [physicists Richard] Garwin and [Sidney] Drell were
unable to elicit interest in their idea from either the Carter or the Reagan Administrations. . . . R. James Woolsey, a former under secretary of the Navy . . . adds that
SUM [shallow underwater missile] was disliked by the Pentagon because, as a complement to Trident, it would require substantial expansion of the Navy's strategic
responsibilities, threatening its role as a force in conventional conflicts." "Why SUM
Didn't Add Up," *Science* 216 (May 21, 1982): 832.

tion seems to arise from the intersection of three forces: (1) the interests of groups in society, (2) the intellectual convictions of experts and policymakers, and (3) comparative knowledge, usually carried in the heads of experts or subject-matter specialists, knowledge of the ways in which problems have been previously handled elsewhere.[20] Which of these animated the production of alternatives in each of our cases? For Medicare, the Council of Economic Advisers and the Peace Corps, there already existed prototypes and models abroad. No doubt part of the reason these social inventions survived over relatively long periods of incubation in the United States was the certain knowledge that in some form or another they could work.

Whereas comparative experience provided the intellectual basis for the invention and incubation of alternatives in type B innovation, for civilian control of atomic energy, the Community Action Programs, and the Truman Doctrine—our three cases of acute innovation—there was much less experience to go on. There were, however, very powerful intellectual convictions that something had to be done, and that the invented alternative at hand was satisfactory and had the overwhelming virtue of being available. The results in all three of these subject areas have given at least some segments of American society second thoughts. Civilian control of atomic energy has proven the least problematic; this may be related to the fact that it received the most explicit public consideration at the time of its

20. As Herbert Simon says, an individual specialist located in technical groups in bureaucracies or in their associated professions "attends to the parts of [the] environment from which innovations may emerge that can be adopted or adapted; he is a principal channel of cultural diffusion within his specialty from other jurisdictions and from the sources of new research and development." Herbert A. Simon, "The Changing Theory and Changing Practice of Public Administration," in Ithiel de Sola Pool, ed., *Contemporary Political Science* (New York: McGraw-Hill, 1967), p. 106. Rufus Browning's study of two state-level bureaucracies leads to similar conclusions: "The main sources of new policies . . . are the members of several professions, usually working in a non-industrial context—in universities, in private non-profit . . . institutions . . . in government agencies in the . . . field in other states, in the federal government, and in other countries." Rufus P. Browning, "Innovation and Non-Innovation Decision Processes in Government Budgeting," in Ira Sharkansky, ed., *Policy Analysis in Political Science* (Chicago: Markham, 1970), p. 318.

adoption. The Truman Doctrine and the Community Action Programs have from time to time since their enactment provoked more controversy.

As for interest groups and their interests, these operate through agents, typically "experts" who focus routinely not on problems of organizational management, but on the cultivation of policy-related ideas. This is evidently true for many sorts of groups: conventional interest-group organizations like the United Auto Workers or the American Medical Association, governmental organizations like the Department of the Army or the Bureau of the Budget, and less well-entrenched organized groups like the Chicago atomic scientists or the National Planning Association. All three types had or developed sufficient internal decision-making structure and self-consciousness to sponsor alternatives that reflected a conception of group interest that could be translated into public policy demands.

It is less fashionable nowadays in political science than it once was to attend to "groups."[21] These are nevertheless meaningful entities when they embody and express interests, and when these interests form the basis for the invention of a policy alternative.

3. POLITICAL CRISIS AND THE POTENTIAL FOR POLICY INNOVATION

I now wish to turn to a fuller consideration of ways in which alternatives, once they are invented, are conveyed to policymakers. This interface is the province of policy entrepreneurs and of would-be sponsors of innovation. Some of our findings bear directly upon the problems faced by persons who want to see changes of various kinds in American public policy.

21. See, however, the classic statement by David B. Truman, *The Governmental Process* (New York: Knopf, 1953); J. David Greenstone, "Group Theories," in Fred I. Greenstein and Nelson W. Polsby, eds., *Handbook of Political Science* 2 (Reading, Mass.: Addison-Wesley, 1975), pp. 243–318; Robert H. Salisbury, "Interest Groups," in *Handbook* 4: 171–228; and the most successful application in contemporary political science of transactional analysis, rooted in group theory, in Raymond Bauer, Ithiel de Sola Pool, and Lewis Anthony Dexter, *American Business and Public Policy* (New York: Atherton, 1963).

The cases, for example, afford an interesting insight into the relationship between "crisis" and "improvisation."[22] Crises may be regarded as situations defined by decision-makers for whatever reasons, but frequently as a response to some notable, well-publicized, exogenous event, as demanding quick decisions. Thus they are characterized by short elapsed time between identification of a "problem" and enactment of a measure to meet the problem. There is some question, however, to what extent crisis decisions are necessarily improvised. Clearly they sometimes are, in which case the invention and search stages are unified. However they need not be; crisis evokes search behavior from decision-makers. If already existing alternatives—even well worked-out alternatives, that is, plans—seem to meet their needs, these alternatives, in adapted form or not, will be pressed into service.

Crises can be situations in which the need to act is so great that measures are enacted even when no remotely sensible alternatives are available, in which case improvisation consists of finding a substantive pretext so that action can be seen to be taken. But the empirical difference between an urgent need to act and the capacity to invent alternatives also creates a set of opportunities for those who are prepared: hence there is utility in one common political strategy in America, namely, attempts by sponsors of ready-made alternatives to coerce feelings of urgency among decision-makers, to invent "crises."[23]

Crises are in this conception a social product. They have to be recognized as such and, from the perspective of the policy entrepreneur, managed. This is especially true when crises do not exist only

22. See also William Solesbury's discussion in "Issues and Innovations in Environmental Policy in Britain, West Germany, and California," *Policy Analysis* 2 (Winter 1976): 1–38; and James Q. Wilson, "Innovation in Organization: Notes Toward a Theory," in James D. Thompson, ed., *Approaches to Organizational Design* (Pittsburgh, Pa.: University of Pittsburgh Press, 1966), pp. 208–209.

23. A relatively recent example of an attempt to create such a feeling of urgency was the twenty-three-page memorandum to President-elect Ronald Reagan from two Republican congressmen, Jack Kemp and David Stockman, promising "an economic Dunkirk" unless heroic measures were taken to end oil price controls, reduce federal spending, provide tax relief, and block the imposition of new regulations on business. Excerpts from this memorandum were printed in the *New York Times* on December 14, 1980.

within the confines of an agency, but are more widely defined as emergencies. Publics then become superattentive to events and to leaders.[24] In crisis situations publics may express generalized needs to be led, but evidently care less about the contents, direction, or consequences of the policies pursued. Crises are highly projective: they are strong stimuli, but ambiguous, and people tend to interpret them as confirmatory of their preexisting prejudices, if they have any strong preexisting prejudices remotely applicable.

For many people, of course, especially leaders, crises create opportunities: expectations are high, rank-and-file citizens are uncommonly receptive to new ideas—or equally to the new enactment of old ideas. Leaders can fill the cognitive vacuum with concrete proposals that often enough have a decent chance of passing, once the basic thoughts are sufficiently familiar. This is one reason why keeping ideas "in the air" sometimes pays off.

A crisis can obtain attention for a "need" and even can get a policy enacted, but it cannot make the policy actually work afterward. Thus people who adopt the innovation strategy of exploiting a crisis have to be reasonably confident of the efficacy of the alternative they promote—or they may get what they "want" and find it was not worth getting. It is frequently beyond the resources of would-be innovators to provoke a crisis in the American body politic, however, so this alternative is of doubtful utility to most citizens. This is also true because the problem of guiding governmental responses to crises into proper channels is frequently as monumental as is the problem of provoking a crisis to begin with.

There is, however, the somewhat less costly alternative of attempting to piggyback on or ride a crisis that occurs exogenously. This is not a game for amateurs, since nearly every interest group that plausibly

24. This phenomenon of heightened attention is almost certainly the underlying mechanism of the "rally round the flag" effect that boosts the short run popular approval ratings of United States Presidents in times of crisis in foreign affairs, as is frequently noted by students of public opinion. See John Mueller, *War, Presidents, and Public Opinion* (New York: John Wiley, 1973), pp. 208–213; Nelson W. Polsby, *Congress and the Presidency*, 3d ed. (Englewood Cliffs, N.J.: Prentice-Hall, 1975), p. 66; and Polsby, "The Democratic Nomination," in Austin Ranney, ed., *The American Elections of 1980* (Washington, D.C.: American Enterprise Institute, 1981), pp. 45–46.

can do so will attempt to capitalize on the feelings of urgency that crises evoke. The most successful example of crisis management for policy innovation in national politics of which I am aware was the concerted and largely successful effort made by those interested in vastly increased aid to higher education to capitalize on the Russian launching of Sputnik in October of 1957.

The fact that Sputnik spurred our primary space effort is from the standpoint of the student of policy initiation an expected outcome, since anybody can see the connection between the Soviet space effort and the United States space effort. The task of leading official thinking to make a connection between the perceived "threat" of imminent Soviet space exploration and inadequate funding of schools and colleges is of a different order of complexity, and suggests that entrepreneurial talent of a very high order was at work.[25]

In contrast, consider the bumbling and disarray of interest groups supporting gun control after the assassination of John F. Kennedy— and once again after the successive assassinations of Martin Luther King and Robert Kennedy seven years later. It is amazing to think that after crises of this character no meaningful federal gun-control

25. In this case the most important incubators were Senator Lister Hill of Alabama and his Alabama colleague, Representative Carl Elliott. Hill was chairman of the Senate Committee on Labor and Elliott was an influential member of the House Education and Labor Committee, and later of the Rules Committee. See Barbara Barksdale Clowse, *Brainpower for the Cold War: The Sputnik Crisis and the National Defense Education Act of 1958* (Westport, Conn.: Greenwood Press, 1981). A recent newspaper interview with Elliott in retirement confirms a picture of an incubated innovation piggybacking on a crisis that by now should be entirely familiar:

Elliott was trying to push the [National Defense Education Act] bill when Harry Truman was president, but was unable to enlist Truman's support.

"I never will forget how he looked at me and said, "Now, Carl, that's a good idea, but it's ahead of its time. Get you something else to work on. . . .

"Eisenhower, while a good man, was not very keen on education matters. I spent a lot of time with the president and his friends trying to sell [the bill] to Eisenhower."

The principle of the bill was not accepted until 1957 when Elliott and other congressmen were conducting a series of meetings across the country.

"What really gave it the boost it needed was when Russia launched Sputnik I. All of a sudden, the best show in town was our education hearings."

Ted Bryant, "Carl Elliott: His Legislation Helped Millions Go to College," *Birmingham Post-Herald*, May 24, 1982.

regulations were put on the books. But this curious fact serves to underscore the central point, which is that crises have to be managed to produce innovations, and the skills involved are probably beyond the resources of most would-be innovators to command.

There remain, however, a number of more promising possibilities. We have spoken of the routine demands of the system for innovation: Presidents needing programs, candidates needing ideas that they can convert into proposals. Both in some measure therefore need policy entrepreneurs who specialize in identifying problems and finding solutions. This must be near to what the Washington-based election analyst Richard Scammon meant when he said:

> There really aren't any new solutions. There are modifications, adjustments. Most good ideas have already been thought of. You don't really come in . . . with a totally new concept. You improve this, polish up that. You take a plan that was discarded four years ago, and you pull it out and look at it. And maybe you salvage Points One, Eleven, and Twenty-nine.[26]

This statement, with its four-year recycling pattern, acknowledges an important symbiosis between political leaders and policy entrepreneurs. In the heat of a presidential campaign, or when a newly inaugurated President wants a "new" program, desk drawers fly open all over Washington. Pet schemes are fished out, dusted off, and tried out on the new political leaders.

The nature of the symbiosis may be hinted at in the following formula:

1. Politicians, because of the requirement that they appeal periodically to electorates, need to identify and to be identified with issues. Policy entrepreneurs supply these issues, these matters to be concerned about, plus the technical back-up for alternative solutions.
2. Entrepreneurs need allies to move their preferred alternatives from incubation to enactment. Thus political leaders help them to reach their goals. In exchange for help in enacting policies of

26. William Whitworth, "Profiles: One-Man Think Tank," *New Yorker* (September 20, 1969): 58. See also Joel Havemann, "Executive Report: Call for Fresh Initiatives Produces Mostly Old Ideas," *National Journal* (June 22, 1974): 921– 924.

which they approve, policy entrepreneurs yield up public credit, which politicians need in order to survive in their election-dependent world.

This often gives the illusion to the inattentive that powerful rather than knowledgeable people are the inventors of public policy. The case studies suggest, however, that policy innovations tend to belong to people who take an interest in them. There is a fallacy that imputes to the occupants of very powerful roles a capacity to attend to everything upon which they *could* have an impact, if they were in fact attentive to it. But at the initiation stage, powerful people are almost always distracted elsewhere. Later on, when initiation moves to enactment, decision-makers will focus on an innovation and in exchange for their attentiveness receive credit; this is a transaction necessary in a society where multiple agreements are needed for enactment, where alternatives are many and time is scarce, and where leaders who intend to stay in office must appeal to masses of people who are both distant and ill-informed. The transfer of credit is thus politically necessary. But it does not change the facts of the initiation process as it can be perceived by close observers.

Innovations may or may not be—and usually are not—at the focus of a decision-maker's attention. Peripheral influence by the most important actors in the political system leaves center stage to less important figures, and brings into focus a whole stratum of actors without whom the business of policymaking could not possibly be accomplished. Such actors include policy entrepreneurs who, by the skillful mobilization of substantive justifications and the accurate identification and thoughtful cultivation of allies, can and do bring new policy into being.

4. IN CONCLUSION

Much of what I have written here has been exploratory, tentative, and speculative. A few general conclusions, however, do seem to me justified on the basis of the ground we have thus far covered in the exploration of the policy initiation process. First, as to methods. We have grounds for believing that political innovation in America is a phenomenon separable from other aspects of political life, with preconditions, contours, and consequences of its own that have only begun to be mapped. What we have learned so far can be subjected to scrutiny, correction, and expansion in many directions. If it is, I am confident that the study of policy initiation can be put on as firm an empirical footing as the study of policy enactment, or of administrative implementation.

Second, and of greater substance, we have learned that what we normally think of as political innovation can be described as a combination of two processes. The first, the process of invention, causes policy options to come into existence. This is the domain of interest groups and their interests, of persons who specialize in acquiring and deploying knowledge about policies and their intellectual convictions, of persons who are aware of contextually applicable experiences of foreign nations, and of policy entrepreneurs, whose careers and ambitions are focused on the employment of their expertise and on the elaboration and adaptation of knowledge to problems. The second process is a process of systemic search, a process that senses and responds to problems, that harvests policy options and turns them to the purposes, both public and career-related, of politicians and public officials. As we have seen, in the American political system, search processes can be activated by exogenously generated crises and by constitutional routines, by bureaucratic needs and by political necessities. Describing political innovation in any particular instance thus entails describing how these two processes interact.[27]

Finally, a point that mixes strategy and substance. I think the study of policy initiation has progressed far enough for us to suspect that an enlightened view of the process must adopt very generous time perspectives. Innovation in American politics is not always the work of a day, and the pursuit of successful innovation is consequently

---

27. This conclusion can probably be generalized to other sorts of innovation. See Rogers, *Diffusion of Innovations*. Stephen E. Toulmin says: "Science develops . . . as the outcome of a double process: at each stage, a pool of competing intellectual variants is in circulation, and in each generation a selection process is going on, by which certain of these variants are accepted and incorporated into the science concerned, to be passed on to the next generation of workers as integral elements of the tradition." Toulmin, "The Evolutionary Development of Natural Science," *American Scientist* 55 (December 1967): 465.

often not a task for those who need quick gratification.[28] Possibly the commonest mistake made by observers and participants who favor innovation is to give up too soon, to measure gains only in the very short run, to become discouraged and to be tempted by tactics that are momentarily gratifying, but self-destructive over the medium term. Those who value innovation, and who wish to preserve and promote the capacity of the American political system to innovate successfully, should ponder this well. If they do, I believe they will come to value not only those persons and events that rock the boat, that increase the pressures upon decision-makers to act, but also those persons who think deeply about problems, who search for and invent alternatives, and who keep alternative solutions alive and available to decision-makers. These relatively quiet figures—inventors, adaptors, policy entrepreneurs, brokers, incubators—are, I believe, less appreciated than they might be, and the tasks they perform less well understood than they should be. For if we look closely enough, and trace far enough back, we may occasionally find that it is on the energy and ingenuity of just such persons that the capacity of a complex society to adapt and meet new needs depends. And upon them also not infrequently rests the task of creating the indispensable substance that the political process processes.

28. An interesting discussion of analogues from the fields of scientific and cultural innovation is Liam Hudson, "The Eureka Syndrome," *Times Higher Education Supplement* (June 11, 1982): 13–14.

Index